Critical Guides to French Texts

Critical Guides to French Texts

EDITED BY ROGER LITTLE, WOLFGANG VAN EMDEN, DAVID WILLIAMS

RABELAIS

Tiers Livre, Quart Livre, Ve Livre

Ian R. Morrison

Lecturer in French
University of Newcastle upon Tyne

Grant & Cutler Ltd
1994

© Grant & Cutler Ltd
1994
ISBN 0 7293 0374 8

I.S.B.N. 84-401-2125-3

DEPÓSITO LEGAL: V. 4.730 - 1994

Printed in Spain by
Artes Gráficas Soler, S. A. - La Olivereta, 28 - 46018 Valencia
for
GRANT & CUTLER LTD
55-57 GREAT MARLBOROUGH STREET, LONDON W1V 2AY

Contents

Contents

Preface

REFERENCES containing italicized arabic numerals indicate items in the Bibliography at the end of this volume. For the *Tiers Livre* (*TL*), I refer to *1*, the edition by Pierre Michel, Collection Folio (Paris, Gallimard, 1966), which is relatively cheap and handy. For the *Quart Livre* (*QL*) and the *Ve Livre* (*VL*), I use volume II of *4*, Rabelais's *Oeuvres complètes* edited by Pierre Jourda, 2 vols (Paris, Garnier, 1962). Thus '*QL*, ch. 37, p. 148' means *Quart Livre,* chapter 37 (*4,* vol. II), p. 148.

Some material on pp. 28-30, below, comes, slightly modified, from a previous paper, 'Pleading, Deciding and Judging in Rabelais' in *Rabelais in Glasgow,* edited and published by J. A. Coleman and Christine M. Scollen-Jimack (Glasgow, 1984), pp. 55-70. I am grateful to the editors for permission to use this material. I am indebted to the University of Newcastle upon Tyne for a term's study-leave in 1986 to work on this book. Above all, I am indebted to Professor van Emden for his help and encouragement.

1

Introduction

Bᴇᴛᴡᴇᴇɴ Rabelais's books there are similarities and divergences. Because of the divergences, the content of the *Tiers Livre* and the *Quart Livre* is considered in separate chapters (2 and 3). However, I obviously make cross-references between the two works; when they treat topics similarly, I give reduced coverage in chapter 3. Current academic opinion suggests that the *Ve Livre* is a collection of rough drafts, not a finished work; as it raises specific problems requiring a different approach, I examine it separately in chapter 4. The art of the *Tiers Livre* and the *Quart Livre* is considered in chapter 5; the *Ve Livre* is excluded because of its unfinished state.

The books uphold, implicitly or explicitly, various values, which, as a rule, I simply ascribe to the text itself, rather than the author. Little is known of the views of the real-life Rabelais, and it is unsafe to assume that they coincided with the values promoted by the texts. Whenever it is necessary to mention the real-life Rabelais, I refer to him by name.

The other term requiring comment is 'narrator'. In all three texts, a narrator recounts the heroes' doings and, mainly in the Prologues, addresses us in the first person. He is named as 'l'autheur, M. François Rabelais' (*TL*, Prologue, p. 61. Cf. *QL*, Prologue, p. 11, and *VL*, Prologue, p. 277). The narrator participates personally in several episodes. But, since some are blatant fantasy, e.g. the 'parolles gelées' (*QL*, chs 55-56), it is impossible to identify the narrator with Rabelais himself, whatever the Prologues may say. The implication for our analysis of content is that the narrator is best regarded as a fictional character and that his judgments, though they must be weighed seriously, need not have overriding authority. I shall return to the narrator's status in chapter 5.

2

The Tiers Livre (1546)

IN the *Tiers Livre*, the character Panurge tries to decide whether to marry. The book is both a comic treatment of Panurge and a carrier for religious and moral themes, as the following outline may indicate. The Prologue foreshadows two themes, *pantagrue-lisme* and the search for enlightenment. Chapters 1-8 introduce Pantagruel and Panurge: the former, in settling the land of Dipsodie, appears a wise ruler (ch. 1); but Panurge, who debates with him various topics such as spending and debt (chs 2-5), seems merely argumentative and idiosyncratic.

In chapters 9-38, the heart of the work, Panurge consults others about his possible marriage. The consultations are of two kinds: some aim to divine what is fated to befall Panurge (chs 10-14, 16-20, 24-25, 37-38); others simply offer him prudential or moral advice (ch. 9, part of 10, 21, 26-28, 29-36). The consultations tend to shift from divination towards advice, which culminates with the views of a theologian, a doctor, and a philosopher (chs 29-36). Chapters 9-38, then, explore the extent to which a man can know and can shape his own fate. Passages of anti-monastic satire are interwoven (notably in chs 15, 22, and 23).

Chapters 39-44, on Bridoye, concern the difficulty of legal judgments but also, by extension, the perplexities of anyone trying to take a decision. In chapters 45-52, after a brief return to divination, it is decided (ch. 47) to go and consult the Dive Bouteille about Panurge's marriage. The final chapters, touching on preparations for the journey, issue in eulogies of the plant *pantagruelion* and, by association, of Pantagruel.

The work, an accumulation of dialogues and episodes, has little plot. Its unity comes from Panurge's obsession with marriage and from the moral and religious themes centred on his obsession. We shall begin with these themes and then move on to the comedy of Panurge; this is merely a change of emphasis, because the comedy is intimately linked with the themes. Our survey of content will end with satire and the pages on *pantagruelion*.

The obvious starting-point is the Prologue. At first, it is dominated by the story of Diogenes the Cynic in Corinth, when Philip of Macedonia threatened the city. The Corinthians made elaborate preparations to resist (pp. 63-67); after watching silently for some days, Diogenes took the tub in which he lived, knocked it about energetically, and then rolled it up and down a hill (pp. 67-69). On inquiry, he explained that

> à aultre office n'estant pour la republicque employé, il en ceste façon son tonneau tempestoit pour, entre ce peuple tant fervent et occupé, n'estre veu seul cessateur et ocieux ['idle']. (p. 69)

His explanation is barbed. It implies that the Corinthians will be impressed, which can happen only if they accept that his agitation compares to activities such as building defences. But in fact it has no like practical worth; indeed the narrative underlines its futility by an analogy with Sisyphus (p. 69). Diogenes seems to be hinting that the Corinthians are too stupid to tell a useless activity from useful ones. Alternatively, he may be suggesting that the citizens' endeavours and his own *are* equal in value – all being equally pointless. Whichever our reading, he clearly means to mock the Corinthians and thus, implicitly, to judge them. In so far as such judgment is a kind of lesson, it foreshadows a theme central to the work, the imparting and seeking of enlightenment. (I use 'enlightenment' as a handy term to cover both knowledge and understanding.) Equally notable is Diogenes's method. He instructs less by word than by actions, actions which have no immediate practical value, but hold a store of meaning for those able to grasp it. The method has some affinity with one used later by Pantagruel.

The narrator then reviews his own position, which he likens to that of Diogenes: he too, with no military role, prefers activity to idleness (pp. 69-71), and the book itself is his 'tonneau Diogenic' (p. 71). Another resemblance emerges when the narrator declares himself almost persuaded

> que guerre soit en Latin dicte belle [BELLUM] [. . .] par raison qu'en guerre apparoisse toute espèce de bien et beau, soit decelée toute espèce de mal et laidure. (p. 69)

This tentative tribute to an aspect of war indicates that he, like Diogenes, attaches importance to eliciting truth from behind externals, and thus that the quest for enlightenment will be a major theme of the book.

Between Diogenes and the narrator there are also differences. While the Cynic's tub is empty, the narrator claims that his 'tonneau' is full of wine (pp. 77-79); offering entertainment and refreshment, it is more humane in character. Again, Diogenes's conduct implied scorn for his audience, the Corinthians. The narrator, on the contrary, esteems his chosen readers as 'Gens de bien' (p. 79). They are also endowed with *pantagruelisme* (p. 77). Here, the word connotes a quality of generosity. Elsewhere, *pantagruelisme* is a more complex kind of wisdom, associated chiefly with Pantagruel, but mirrored on occasion in the narrator and close companions such as Epistemon. It becomes another main theme of the *Tiers Livre*.

Lastly, the narrator rejects certain other readers: lawyers and, above all, religious hypocrites ('caphars') and monks (pp. 79-81). The 'caphars' and monks may well overlap. In them, he sees potential censors: 'Venez vous icy culletans articuler ['accuse'] mon vin et compisser mon tonneau?' (p. 81). Similarly, he spurns the 'cerveaux à bourlet, grabeleurs de corrections' (p. 79). Scholars usually associate the first expression with doctoral headgear (as when Frere Jean talks of a 'docteur [. . .] à triple bourlet', *QL*, ch. 54, p. 202); 'grabeler' ('to sift') can imply hostile pedantry (cf. the Council to 'grabeler les articles de la foy contre les nouveaulx hoereticques', *QL*, ch. 18, p. 93). Here, then, the text no doubt refers to nit-picking theologians such as those of the Sorbonne, who had assailed Rabelais's earlier writing. Moreover, the narrator condemns the 'caphars' as generally and radically evil: 'ilz ne sont de bien, ains de mal, et de ce mal

duquel journellement à Dieu requerons estre delivrez'; his allusion to the Lord's Prayer indicates how deep their evil runs (p.
81). Vehemently expressed and strategically placed at the end of
the Prologue, these strictures suggest that later satire on churchmen, and possibly on lawyers, will relate to essential values and
not to superficial professional quirks of these groups. This
onslaught also heralds the general importance of religious
questions in the work.

The main religious authorities in the text are Pantagruel and
Hippothadée. Pantagruel's religious views are part of *pantagruelisme*. Hippothadée is a theologian, but not a 'cerveau à bourlet';
Pantagruel endorses him as a good theologian, one concerned to
'planter profundement es cueurs humains la vraye et vive foy
catholicque' (ch. 29, p. 369). If one expression summed up Hippothadée's outlook, it would be, 'Si Dieu plaist'. To him, the
words convey the nothingness of man without God: 'N'est ce
nous declairer [. . .] rien sans luy n'estre, rien ne valoir, rien ne
povoir, si sa saincte grace n'est sus nous infuse?' (ch. 30, p.
377). The result of every single enterprise depends on God's
will: Hippothadée expands, 'N'est ce [. . .] tout ce que proposons
remettre à ce que sera disposé par sa saincte volunté?' (ib.). Further, in moral matters, it depends on God's will whether men's
very intentions are good or evil. It is Pantagruel who makes the
point explicitly. Men's moral decisions come from their con-
sciences, their 'cœurs et pensées, qui est l'officine ['workshop']
de tout bien et tout mal' (ch. 7, p. 143); men are, then, ultimately
responsible for these decisions. But it is a man's *affection* (here,
a disposition to act in a particular way) that determines on any
occasion whether he opts for good or evil. And a moral choice
will be good only if the *affection* is 'par le esprit munde ['pure']
reiglée'; it will be evil, 'si hors aequité par l'esprit maling est
l'affection depravée' (ib.). These alternatives show a stark belief
in the power of the evil spirit and a corresponding conviction
that men cannot even mean well without divine grace.

If God abandons man, he has neither power nor goodness.
But Hippothadée's exchanges with Panurge indicate that God
does not abandon mankind. He assures Panurge that he will
avoid cuckoldry, if such is God's will. Panurge retorts:

Si Dieu plaist [. . .] Dea, si feust condition à laquelle je peusse obvier, je ne me desespererois du tout ['not . . . entirely']; mais vous me remettez au conseil privé de Dieu. (ch. 30, p. 375)

Believing he can neither know God's will nor influence his own future, he feels helpless. Hippothadée replies that we can readily know God's will (His 'sainctz plaisirs'): 'Le bon Dieu [. . .] nous les a revelez, annoncez, declairez et apertement descriptz par les sacres bibles' (p. 377); and he illustrates by rehearsing biblical precept on how to find a virtuous wife and keep her so (p. 379; see *14*, pp. 74-76). God's will, in this sphere, it is that men try to help themselves by a certain line of conduct. The implications of the passage go beyond marriage, since God's 'sainctz plaisirs' extend to other fields. Hippothadées' view is clearly that, in general, Scripture reveals God's will and that men can help to shape their own fates. But ultimately, of course, the individual still depends on God both for the purity of his own intentions and the success of his efforts. Hippothadée's final words to Panurge recall the point: 'continuellement implorerez la grace de Dieu à vostre protection' (p. 381).

As has been suggested above, to know God's will is to know His commands to all mankind. However, Panurge really wants to discover a different aspect of God's will, namely what, in fact, the future holds for himself. Pantagruel deals with this wish when Panurge first asks whether he would gain by marrying. He answers that the result is 'dependent des fatales dispositions du ciel' and that

Il se y convient mettre à l'adventure [. . .] baissant la teste, baisant la terre et se recommandant à Dieu au demourant [. . .] Aultre asceurance ne vous en sçauroys je donner. (ch. 10, pp. 167-69)

The last sentence indicates that no man can scrutinize God's providential designs for himself. Before God, the right attitude is not futile curiosity, but entreaty ('se recommandant à Dieu') and humble acceptance of His will ('baissant la teste').

Pantagruel shows a keen sense that man's ultimate concern should be with God, and that all else is correspondingly insignificant. For example, glossing St Paul's advice, 'ceulx qui ont femme soient comme non ayans femme' (I Corinthians VII. 29), he speaks of 'celle unicque et supreme affection que doibt l'homme à Dieu' (ch. 35, p. 429). This does not mean that man should give no thought to earthly things – the wise ruler Pantagruel clearly does – but that he should regard their outcome with a due sense of proportion. This sense, coupled presumably with acceptance of God's will for himself, helps explain Pantagruel's serene view of earthly things, as it emerges for example in his patient dealings with Panurge.

Elsewhere, the text presents his serenity differently. The narrator tells us, 'Jamais ne se tourmentoit, jamais ne se scandalizoit', adding that 'tous les biens que le ciel couvre [. . .] ne sont dignes d'esmouvoir nos affections et troubler nos sens et espritz' (ch. 2, p. 97). This explanation involves a changed perspective: according to the narrator, if Pantagruel had let himself be troubled, he would have been 'forissu du deificque manoir de raison' (ib.) ('must have most grossly abandoned the divine mansion of reason', 6, I, p. 263). Clearly, if there is no common measure between the divine and the earthly, and if reason is somehow god-like, logically, rational man should not be troubled by earthly things. However, this view raises a problem. Hippothadée and Pantagruel himself make much of man's dependence on God; yet the narrator, here at least, gives rationality a status hard to reconcile with total dependence. The tension is not really resolved but, in the last resort, Pantagruel places overriding emphasis on dependence on God. As he reminds the judges of Myrelingues, '[Dieu] veult souvent sa gloire apparoistre en l'hebetation des saiges' (ch. 43, p. 505). For him, true human wisdom includes knowing the limits of reason and human wisdom.

Naturally, *pantagruelisme* concerns relations with men as well as with God. The narrator hopes his readers will judge his work generously: they have the quality of *pantagruelisme*, thanks to which 'Je les ay ordinairement veuz bon vouloir en payement prendre [. . .] quand debilité de puissance y a esté associée' (Prologue, p. 77). *Pantagruelisme*, then, involves an approach to judging men and their doings. If, for the *panta-gruéliste*, 'bon vouloir' is of the essence, he will judge men chiefly by their intentions; the importance which we have seen attached to conscience accords with this approach. It is exemplified in relation to the judge, Bridoye. When called to account for a wrong verdict, he reveals that he decides between litigants merely by casting dice. In defending Bridoye, Pantagruel stresses his weaknesses, namely age and 'simplesse' (ch. 43, p. 505). Later, Epistemon talks of his good intentions, his 'affection syncere', in resorting to dice, because he distrusted his own 'sçavoir et capacité' to do justice; and Epistemon speculates that Bridoye's verdicts have so often proved just, despite his methods, because the heavens looked kindly on his intentions (ch. 44, pp. 511-13). However, Bridoye himself voiced no such diffidence, but claimed to follow normal judicial practice in using dice (e.g. ch. 39, pp. 467, 471). Epistemon simply ignores Bridoye's expressed, aberrant view, and unilaterally credits him with an unexpressed, worthy motive, which tends to excuse his behaviour.

Epistemon's comments illustrate two points. First, the *panta-gruéliste* so respects conscience that he will give credit for good intentions, even if they involve a mistaken view of things. Secondly, the *pantagruéliste* ascribes actions to the best motive imaginable; Pantagruel himself 'tout acte interpretoit à bien' (ch. 2, p. 97). The case shows, too, how sharply judgment on a man may be distinguished from judgment on his actions. Bridoye's conduct is condemned, both for its inherent character (his procedure is improper and his verdict unjust), and for its consequences (the victim of his verdict has suffered loss). On the first point, Pantagruel proposes that Bridoye no longer sit alone, but be guided by another judge in his 'procedures judiciaires' (ch. 43, p. 507); on the second, he undertakes to ensure compensation of the party harmed by Bridoye's verdict (ch. 43, p. 505). Thus, a benign judgment on Bridoye himself is possible without hiding the wrong which he has done.

This lucid tolerance prompts two further comments. First, it is presumably linked with charity. Typically, in rebutting Panurge's praise of debts, Pantagruel cites St Paul's injunction, 'Rien [. . .] à personne ne doibvez fors amour et dilection mutuelle' (ch. 5, p. 129). Secondly, the tolerance of the *panta-grueliste* has limits. It excludes the radically evil, those whom we have seen the narrator reject from his readership in the Pro-logue (p. 81). They are of course the targets of various satirical assaults in the *Tiers Livre*.

Pantagruel has the main role in articulating the book's moral themes and some of its religious ones. But Panurge, to whom we now turn, bulks larger, for his hesitations over marriage occupy most of the work. His recourse to divination is important for the questions how far men can know or influence their own futures, and it particularly complements his debate with Hippothadée on these subjects. Panurge's experience suggests that divination is radically unsatisfactory. No method seems able to give clear, trustworthy answers. Pantagruel rejects two (using dice and knucklebones) as diabolical deceptions (ch. 11, p. 177). (On div-ination by dice, see *10*, pp. 136-37.) Other methods, though less tainted, are also unreliable. Sometimes, as in divination by dreams, the seer's own insight may be blurred (ch. 13, p. 197). Sometimes oracular expression misleads: Pantagruel says that many have been deluded 'tant à cause des [. . .] obscuritez des motz, que de la briefveté des sentences', and that consequently oracles expressed 'par gestes et par signes estoient les plus veri-tables et certains estimez' (ch. 19, p. 259). But is gesture clearer than words? Panurge agrees to consult, 'par gestes' a deaf-mute, preferably male. (On dumb prophets, see *10*, p. 141.) He ex-plains his preference by telling the story of the deaf-mute Verona who, when asked the way by a young Roman, took his gestures for an amorous proposition. Panurge intends to show that women will place erotic constructions on all gestures (ch. 19, p. 263); but, whatever his purpose, the anecdote suggests that signs, like words, can be ambiguous.

In practice, however the prophecies are expressed, Pantagruel and Panurge disagree about their import: Panurge interprets them favourably, while Pantagruel concludes that Panurge's wife will cuckold, beat, and rob him (e.g. ch. 12, pp. 183, 189, 191; ch. 14, p. 211; ch. 18, p. 247; ch. 20, p. 277). Pantagruel's status gives his opinions weight. Others share his view of Panurge's fate: e.g. Epistemon (ch. 18, p. 255), and the astrologer Her Trippa (ch. 25, p. 321). No-one agrees with Panurge. But whatever the balance of opinion, it is, and can only be a matter of opinion. This follows from Pantagruel's own belief that divination is uncertain, and naturally he never claims that Panurge's misfortune is assured. (It has indeed been argued [in *11*] that Panurge's interpretations often seem as sound as Pantagruel's.)

Uncertainty is one defect of divination. But, if it achieves even apparent probability, it can take on another more sinister defect. If an oracle did reveal things which are fated to happen, they would have to be regarded as inevitable. A discussion between Panurge and Frere Jean highlights this truism (chs 26-28). Panurge momentarily admits fearing that, for him, cuckoldry is unavoidable: 'tous [. . .] afferment qu'il me est ainsi praedestiné des cieulx' (ch. 28, p. 353). Frere Jean offers no escape, but echoes Panurge's fears in jocular astrological terms, 'puis qu'ainsi t'est praedestiné, voudroys tu faire retrograder les planetes' (p. 361). The point is not to suggest that a mode of divination, here astrology, does after all offer certainty; Frere Jean is too minor a character and his remarks too flippant to make such a point with authority. The focus is rather on Panurge's frame of mind: having turned to divination for reassurance, and instead met threats of woe, he falls into a mood of anguished helplessness. Her Trippa's predictions leave him 'fasché' and 'matagrabolisé ['stunned']' (ch. 26, p. 333), and he is frustrated that Frere Jean is no help (ch. 28, p. 361). The placing of the account of Panurge's anguish is significant: it is a prelude and foil to Hippothadée's advice (ch. 30). The contrast between divination and Revelation is total: whereas oracular pronouncements are shown first to be unclear and then to be sinisterly enervating as well, the Word of God, according to Hippothadée, is clear and prompts the hearer to act.

But does this conclusion exhaust the subject of divination? It fills many pages, and Pantagruel and Epistemon seem too well informed (e.g. chs 10, 24) to have only a casual interest in it. Let us reconsider how divination is introduced. Pantagruel tells Panurge that the outcome of his marriage depends on 'fatales dispositions du ciel', adding, 'Aultre asceurance ne vous en sçauroys je donner' (ch. 10, pp. 167-69). Then, oddly, he himself initiates the efforts to divine Panurge's future. Three remarks are possible.

First, Pantagruel's inconsistency is only apparent. *Asceurance* means 'certainty'. As he doubts the efficacity of divination, he expects no 'asceurance' from it; but that view is quite compatible with trying divination, open-mindedly, to see whether it may nonetheless give some hints. His remarks on the so-called sibyl are revealing. Epistemon, fearing witchcraft, is loath to visit her. Pantagruel replies that, even if she is no sibyl, consulting her is harmless; and he goes on, 'Que nuist sçavoir tousjours et tousjours apprendre, feust ce d'un sot [. . .] d'une pantoufle' (ch. 16, p. 231). Knowledge, then, is worth pursuing, however unlikely the prospective source. Here, perhaps more than anywhere else in the book, it is clear that Panurge's search for personal guidance is subsumed under the larger theme of the quest for enlightenment.

A second point is that personal affection encourages Pantagruel in this open-minded approach, since he wishes to assuage Panurge's doubts. When about to suggest consulting the sibyl, he says, 'L'amour que je vous porte inveteré [. . .] me sollicite de penser à vostre bien' (ch. 16, p. 229). He goes as far as he can to consult oracles in ways likely to satisfy Panurge. Thus, though he firmly rejects Panurge's idea of divining with dice, he instead proposes using dice indirectly, i.e. in order to select lines from Virgil, so that these latter may serve as a basis for divination:

> Pour toutesfoys vous satisfaire, bien suys d'advis que jectez troys dez sus ceste table. Au nombre des poinctz advenens nous prendrons les vers du feueillet que aurez ouvert. (ch. 11, p. 179)

Such concessions to Panurge's foibles may of course be attributed not only to affection but also to *pantagruelisme* with its compassion for human weakness.

The third remark on Pantagruel and divination concerns the possible parallel between him and Diogenes. At Corinth, Diogenes throws himself knowingly into futile activity; Pantagruel takes the lead in consulting oracles, which he believes futile, to the extent that no certainty will emerge. Admittedly, their intentions diverge: Diogenes means to mock the citizens, Pantagruel to help his old companion, either by finding some hint of his future or, preferably, by persuading him to abandon divination and decide for himself. (See ch. 29, p. 367 and, below, p. 23.) But the two cases are similar in that practically vain acts are charged with intellectual significance, which may escape the immediate participants (the Corinthians, Panurge), but is clear enough to the reader. The consultations undertaken at Pantagruel's behest serve by their outcome as a critique of divination in itself and of the dangerous credulity shown by those who turn to it. Despite repeated failures to obtain an answer to his liking, Panurge does not learn the lesson, but it is plain to the reader. And if Pantagruel's methods recall Diogenes's, the parallel helps distance the narrator himself from any apparent advocacy of divination: to show Diogenes rolling his tub manifestly does not imply in the narrator a belief in the inherent value of tub-rolling; likewise, to show Pantagruel initiating recourse to divination does not imply in the narrator a belief in the intrinsic worth of divination.

The underlying attitude, sceptical curiosity about divination, seems fairly typical of the period. For centuries, the Church had routinely condemned it, whether for its deterministic implications, which threatened the notion of free will (especially in the case of astrology), or for its demonic associations. Similar hostility was found among the Reformers, as in Calvin's *Advertissement contre l'Astrologie judiciaire* (1548?). On the other hand, this was a time of curiosity about divination, linked at least partly with the rediscovery of the ancient world, in which many divinatory practices had originated. Moreover, the very intensity of some condemnations, such as Calvin's *Advertissement*, suggests that interest in divination was practical and not merely academic. Panurge's quandary, then, provides the occasion for comic treatment of a topical question. (On astrology, see *12*, Introduction; on divination in general and in the *Tiers Livre,* see *10*, chs 5-6.)

Panurge's fears of marriage are connected with contemporary views about women. Misogyny was common, and often took the specific form of hostility to marriage (*14*, pp. 5-11). The *Tiers Livre* does not have the latter feature. Pantagruel regards marital bliss as a real possibility: 'Nous voyons bon nombre de gens tant heureux [. . .] qu'en leur mariage, semble reluire quelque idée et repraesentation des joyes de paradis' (ch. 10, p. 167). True, he also thinks that marriage can be torment (ib.). Crucially, however, he does not try to dissuade Panurge from marrying, and is himself ready to marry a wife chosen by his father (ch. 48, pp. 539-41).

Although marriage in general receives at least muted approval in the text, individual women characters are treated unfavourably. They are neither prominent nor often shown in a wholly good light: e.g. the sibyl is grotesque (ch. 17), and the woman of Smyrna homicidal, even if there is some excuse for her actions (ch. 44; see pp. 32-33, below). In practice the view of women which bulks largest in the *Tiers Livre* is that expressed mainly by Rondibilis the doctor. He concedes that chaste women do exist, but holds that, physiologically, most have rampant sexual appetites (ch. 32, p. 401); husbands, not always being able to content their wives, are 'en danger perpetuel d'estre coquz' (p. 403). Women's other alleged hallmark is perversity. According to Hippothadée, some theologians believe that Eve ate the forbidden fruit, only because it was forbidden (ch. 33, p. 413).

Panurge agrees that failure to satisfy wives' appetites is 'cause unicque, de faire les maris coquz' (ch. 14, p. 213). Moreover, his own virility must be waning with age, as Frere Jean observes (ch. 28, p. 351). Given his own subjective views of women, Panurge cannot but fear cuckoldry.

His fear is aggravated because, having cuckolded others, he risks repayment in kind: Pantagruel says, after Seneca, 'ce qu'à aultruy tu auras faict, soys certain qu'aultruy te fera' (ch. 9, p. 161). Though Panurge seems at first to shrug off the warning, he is receptive to such threats because he generally presumes ill of others. His cynicism emerges, for example, when the dying Raminagrobis complains of 'pestilentes bestes, noires [. . .] grivolées' (ch. 21, p. 285). Panurge thinks his complaint refers to members of religious orders with their variously coloured habits. Epistemon replies that it may refer literally to insects, and adds the general point that 'Il faut tousjours de son presme ['neighbour'] interpreter toutes choses à bien' (ch. 22, p. 293). But Panurge scoffs, 'Aprenez moy [. . .] à congnoistre mousches en laict! Il [Raminagrobis] est [. . .] haereticque' (ch. 22, pp. 293-95). In systematically presuming well of his neighbour, Epistemon shows *pantagruelisme*; in dismissing his outlook, Panurge acts as a kind of *anti-pantagrueliste*. Thus his cynical distrust both exacerbates his marital fears and also makes him a foil to the *pantagruelistes*.

Why, dreading cuckoldry, does he even consider marriage? He mentions four reasons to Pantagruel: to escape solitude; to satisfy his own sexual appetites safely; to have someone to nurse him in sickness; and to have legitimate issue (ch. 9, pp. 161-65). With the possible exception of the last, his reasons are not put in terms of positive advantage, but are expressed negatively, as ways of avoiding the disadvantages of not marrying: e.g. if he does not marry, he will be lonely. Objectively, it matters little whether reasons are stated as advantages gained or disadvantages avoided. But Panurge's use of the second formulation is significant in the tone it sets and in what it tells us about him: the tone is cheerless; and Panurge envisages continued bachelorhood, as he does marriage, with fear. (In the *Tiers Livre,* the other fear which he mainly shows is that of damnation; this will be considered in connexion with religious satire.) In his fears, he is obviously a foil to the serene Pantagruel.

Another major topic to which Panurge is central is self-knowledge. He is said to lack the quality, for example by Epistemon (ch. 15, p. 227). The defect emerges when Panurge rehearses his competing fears of bachelorhood and of marriage (ch. 9, pp. 161-65). His inability to choose between the two sets of fears shows his want of self-knowledge; when he complains that Pantagruel's answers are inconsistent, Pantagruel retorts 'en vos propositions tant y a de si et de mais, que je n'y sçaurois rien fonder ne rien resouldre. N'estez vous asceuré de vostre vouloir?' (ch. 10, p. 167). Those whom Panurge asks for advice (rather than divination) usually stress the need for self-knowledge, e.g. Hippothadée (ch. 30, pp. 373-75). Pantagruel himself reads Raminagrobis's poem to mean that 'en l'entreprinse de mariage chascun doibt estre arbitre de ses propres pensées, et de soy mesmes conseil prendre. Telle a tousjours esté mon opinion' (ch. 29, p. 367). Self-knowledge is not advocated for its own

sake, but as a prerequisite for making personal decisons. This repeated advice implies first that Panurge must take responsibility
for his own decisions in this prudential sphere, just as he would
in the strictly moral sphere. It also implies that self-knowledge is
a major aspect of the theme of enlightenment: Panurge's persistent, vain search for guidance from outside dramatizes, page
after page, the point that he should have been seeking guidance
inside himself.

Advocacy of self-knowledge is clearly not an invitation to
mere preoccupation with self or self-love. An essential part of
the comedy of Panurge is that he does combine ignorance of self
with love of self. Pantagruel taxes him explicitly with undue
'amour de soy' (ch. 29, p. 367). The weakness is already clear in
his reasons for contemplating marriage, of which only desire for
legitimate issue is at all disinterested (ch. 9). Among other marks
of his self-love are his boastfulness and ostentation, which lend
themselves particularly to comic treatment.

Typically, he boasts of his virility to Frere Jean (ch. 27, pp.
345-49). But Panurge is ageing; and in order to reconcile his
avowed fear of cuckoldry with his claim to be indefatigably vir-
ile (and so able to satisfy his wife), he ascribes the risk not to
impotence but to absence:

> Gentil compaignon tousjours, autant ou plus que jamais. Je
> ne crains pas cela [. . .] Je crains que par quelque longue ab-
> sence de nostre roy Pantagruel, auquel force est que je face
> compaignie [. . .] ma femme me face coqu. (ch. 28, p. 353)

Unimpressed, the monk counters with a litany of terms evoking
Panurge's enfeebled state: 'couillon flatry, C. moisy . . .' (pp.
355-59), and commends derisively a remedy associated with
another ageing swain, Hans Carvel (pp. 363-65). Elsewhere,
Panurge vaunts his courage. When, for example, Pantagruel
observes that the journey to the Dive Bouteille will be 'plene de
dangiers', he interjects, 'Quels dangiers? [. . .] Les dangiers se
refuyent de moy' (ch. 47, p. 533). But whenever he does meet
danger, real or imaginary, Panurge's behaviour is craven, as in
the sibyl's hovel, which he imagines full of devils: 'Fuyons.

Serpe Dieu, je meurs de paour. Je n'ayme poinct les diables' (ch. 17, pp. 241-43). Whether vaunting his virility or his bravery, Panurge's claims appear empty, and the resultant inconsistencies in his behaviour contribute to the comedy of the character. (As we shall see, Panurge's cowardice is a major feature of the *Quart Livre* [e.g. chs 18-24, 66-67].)

As to ostentation, the clearest example is his adoption of eye-catching, puzzling garb (ch. 7, p. 141), which he explains with apparent relish to Pantagruel. For example, his robe has the form of a toga; the toga being Roman peace-time dress, it signifies that he is not going to war; and that is because he will avail himself of the Mosaic law exempting men from military service for the first year of their marriage (p. 145). The garment advertises, circuitously, an intention to marry. Pantagruel comments that externals such as dress are, morally speaking, neither good nor bad, 'choses [. . .] externes et indifferentes' (ch. 7, p. 143). Though apparently accepting Panurge's dress, this may amount to a rebuke for attaching undue importance to externals. Moreover, Pantagruel criticizes explicitly, though gently, 'la nouveaulté et mespris du commun usaige' (ib.); in short, Panurge's exhibitionism is taken to convey scorn for others. Such contempt seems a natural consequence of his self-love.

Later, Panurge explains his attire differently, saying he has vowed to wear it until he obtains an answer to his doubts over marriage:

> Pourtant ['and so'] ay je faict veu à sainct François le Jeune [. . .] porter lunettes au bonnet, ne porter braguette en chausses, que sus ceste mienne perplexité d'esprit je n'aye eu resolution aperte. (ch. 24, pp. 309-11)

In jest, Epistemon compares this with vows to undertake feats of arms, that is, vows implying heroic determination (ch. 24, p. 311). The irony is clear: Panurge is resolute, but on only one point, that he must have someone or something else make his decision for him. His dress is a show of (unheroic) resolve to hide his dearth of real resolve – in vain, since, according to Epistemon, 'la voix publicque estoit toute consommée en mocqueries de son desguisement' (ch. 24, p. 309).

Panurge's self-love permeates discussion of the predictions about his future. It appears less in his disagreeing with others, for the sense of many predictions may be genuinely debatable, than in his manner. Thus, when Epistemon cites ancient authorities to uphold his opinion about the sibyl, Panurge simply dismisses them as 'folz comme poëtes' (ch. 18, p. 257). This is such arrogance that Pantagruel blames it on diabolical influence, 'L'esprit maling vous seduyt' (ch. 19, p. 259). Later, he tells Panurge, 'philautie et amour de soy vous deçoit ['deceives']' (ch. 29, p. 367). *Philautie* is a kind of self-infatuation which closes Panurge's mind to others' opinions, and prevents the receptiveness to truth advocated by Pantagruel (ch. 16, p. 231). Panurge, while seeming to seek enlightenment, is the very opposite of a real seeker for enlightenment.

Lastly, Panurge's self-love affects his attitude to his fate, whenever he admits to himself that the oracles may portend cuckoldry. Sometimes, as we have seen, his reaction is anguished, but it can also be wilful. Of the lines from Virgil, he concludes, 'je prends ces troys sors à mon grand adventaige. Aultrement j'en appelle' (ch. 12, p. 191). If his fate displeases him, he seeks to reject it. Thus, self-love produces a presumptuous attitude contrasting with yet another facet of *pantagruelisme,* the devout entreaty and humble acceptance commended by Pantagruel in chapter 10.

It is tempting to see Panurge as a mere fool. Indeed Pantagruel, echoing Triboullet, does once call him a 'fol enraigé' for contemplating marriage in old age (ch. 46, p. 525). But Panurge also has eloquence and inventive wit. This is not the place for detailed analysis of the former. It may suffice to mention one example among many, his praise of borrowing and lending (chs 3-4). Though his oratory does not convince Pantagruel, it prompts him to praise Panurge's rhetorical skill (ch. 5, p. 129). As for Panurge's wit, it often appears in the debates about advice and predictions, such as the sibyl's poem. She writes, presumably of Panurge's future wife, 'Engroissera, De toy non' (ch. 17, pp. 243-45). Pantagruel interprets: 'elle vous fera coqu, se abandonnant à aultruy, et par aultruy devenent grosse' (ch. 18, p. 247). Panurge counters, 'Ma femme engroissera [. . .] mais non de moy [. . .] Ce sera d'un beau petit enfantelet qu'elle sera grosse' (p. 249). The crux is the word 'de': does it mean 'by' or 'with'? The latter reading (Panurge's) has the defect of emptying 'De toy non' of significance. If the expression means, in effect, 'with a child', it adds nothing to 'Engroissera'. But even if Panurge's reading is the less plausible, there is some ambiguity in the sibyl's words, and Panurge exploits it resourcefully. (Similar cases occur in chapters 12, 14, and 18.)

Though Panurge often misuses his eloquence and wit, these qualities make him a fascinating character. Moreover, he is undoubtedly presented as a likeable figure, since the other characters hold him in obvious affection: Pantagruel speaks of his 'amour [. . .] inveteré' for Panurge (ch. 16, p. 229); Frere Jean says, 'je t'aime du bon du foye' (ch. 21, p. 283); Epistemon is termed an 'antique amy' (ch. 24, p. 309). Thus, much as Panurge's companions criticize his faults, it is with an affection which encourages a like attitude in the reader.

Turning to satire, we may begin with the religious orders. They are satirized for gluttony (e.g. ch. 15) and lechery (e.g. ch. 27, p. 347). More radically, satire falls on their perverse values, as exemplified in the tale of Soeur Fessue, the pregnant nun (ch. 19). She alleges rape, but her abbess is suspicious, because the so-called rape happened in the convent dormitory and the nun did not call for help. Soeur Fessue explains that she had not dared, 'pource qu'on dortouoir y a silence sempiternelle' (p. 265), insinuating that the rule of silence had left her helpless. Whether this is simply a ploy to escape punishment is immaterial for present purposes. What matters is the conflict between the monastic rule and the law of God, and the evidence that, in such cases, monastic orders prefer their own rules: tellingly, the abbess says, not that the nun should have called out despite the rule, but that she should have signalled for help. Her reply to this absurd idea is fittingly ludicrous: 'je [. . .] faisois signes du cul tant que povois' (p. 267). For his part, Pantagruel is unamused, soberly concluding, 'toute moinerie moins crainct les commandemens de Dieu transgresser que leurs statutz provinciaulx' (ib.).

Both by exposure to ridicule and by grave, express condemnation, the monastic scale of values is satirized as sacrilegiously twisted.

Equally sinister are the religious orders' dealings with the laity. Panurge identifies as mendicants the 'pestilentes bestes' that harass Raminagrobis on his death-bed (ch. 22, p. 293). The poet deplores their 'fraudulentes poinctures [. . .] forgées en l'officine de ne sçay quelle insatiabilité' (ch. 21, p. 285). Plainly, they are dishonest and rapacious. Worse, they seek gain by coming between the faithful and God, distracting Raminagrobis from contemplation of the 'bien et felicité que le bon Dieu a praeparé à ses fideles et esleuz' (ch. 21, p. 287). Panurge takes up the same theme, but from the opposite side. He thinks that, as the poet has rebuffed the 'tant beatz peres', they will declare him 'haereticque et damné', but that, if he makes them a bequest, 'Ainsi pourra il de Dieu pardon avoir' (ch. 23, p. 297). Panurge, then, accepts that they can interpose between man and God, and that only if they are satisfied can God pardon man. As we have seen, Panurge is culpably unwilling to take responsibility for his own life, and constantly seeks outside relief from this responsibility. His belief in salvation through buying intermediaries is similarly irresponsible. Obviously, the orders' intrusive pretensions foster and exploit such irresponsibility. And, implicitly, the fact that Panurge is their champion helps discredit them.

Panurge's role here is also to hint that the orders' tyranny is abetted by the submissiveness of the laity, and that the laity submits from mere superstition. Such is his own fear of the devils whom he expects to seize the soul of Raminagrobis, for spurning the mendicants' aid. Though he feels he should go to remonstrate with the poet, Panurge's terror of the Devil stops him. His fear is ridiculed by his own incoherence: 'Le Diable me emport si je y voys. Si je y allois, le Diable me emporteroit' (ch. 23, p. 299). Lay people's part-responsibility for their own spiritual subjection is indicated explicitly by Gargantua. Attacking the canon-law position that a marriage can be valid without the consent of the couple's parents, he assails the 'tirannicque praesumption' of the clerics, 'lesquelz ont dict loix es gens mariez sus le faict de mariage'. But he decries equally 'la superstitieuse stupidité des

gens mariez' in acquiescing (ch. 48, p. 541). (On legal aspects of
these marriages, see *14*, pp. 44-54.)

In summary, then, such failings as gluttony and lechery are
indeed criticized, but remain relatively peripheral; however
inappropriate they may be for churchmen and however much
hypocrisy they may generate, they are themselves ordinary
human weaknesses, and the *pantagrueliste* is tolerant of frailty.
The main thrust of the satire is more damaging. As we have
seen, the outlook of Hippothadée and Pantagruel is God-centred
and encapsulated in the words 'Si Dieu plaist'. Parts of the
Catholic Church, notably the religious orders, are depicted as
seeking to oust God's law and usurp His place. The contrast is
too plain to need explicit statement in the text; juxtaposition is
enough. The crucial religious failings stand in antithesis to *pantagruelisme*, and in that sense cohere perfectly with the theme of
pantagruelisme. It is this thematic coherence which gives the
satire much of its force.

As for legal satire, we find predictable allusions to lawyers'
greed (e.g., ch. 42, p. 493). But litigants too are implicitly cen-
sured through the remarks of Perrin Dendin, the 'apoincteur des
procès' (ch. 41). He succeeded as conciliator by waiting until
disputes were 'biens meurs et digerez' (p. 487). The expression
implies, not that the parties gradually came to see reason, but
that their money ran out, 'declinoient au dernier but de play-
doirie, car leurs bourses estoient vuides' (ib.). Dendin's interven-
tions merely spared the litigants humiliation, 'ceste pernicieuse
honte qu'on eust dict: "Cestuy cy premier s'est rendu; il a premier parlé d'apoinctement" ' (p. 489). As with churchmen's
tyranny over the laity, the satire does not focus solely on the
exploiters, but duly ridicules the exploited as well, this time for
their spendthrift folly and pride.

Other dangers of litigation are embodied in Bridoye, who
tried cases by casting dice (chs 39-42). When challenged, he says
that he is using the *alea judiciorum* ('dice of judgment') (ch. 39,
p. 467). Manifestly, in legal parlance, the words do not refer to
dice but, figuratively, to the element of chance which may enter
into the deciding of cases. Bridoye, however, believes using real
dice is normal judicial practice. His dice, he assures the court of

Myrelingues, are like those 'des quelz [. . .] vous aultres, messieurs, ordinairement usez en ceste vostre Court souveraine, aussi font tous aultres juges, en decision des procès' (p. 467). The obvious satirical point is that real-life courts' decisions, taken conventionally, are haphazard.

Worse is alleged against the court of Myrelingues, which may represent the Parlement de Paris (see *28*). Epistemon attacks the court in a passage so larded with negative particles that I cannot pretend to understand it fully (ch. 44, p. 513). But it is clear, at least, that he terms the judges' hands 'pleines de sang et de perverse affection', implying that wrong decisions arise not only from accident but also from deliberate injustice and cruelty. The force of these strictures is limited, however, because Pantagruel does not associate himself with them, and has indeed shown a benign attitude to the court of Myrelingues (ch. 43, pp. 503-05).

The Bridoye episode prompts other, more radical questions about the ability of the human mind to solve problems of legality and justice, notably in chapter 44, 'Comment Pantagruel raconte une estrange histoire des perplexitez du jugement humain'. The tale concerns a woman whose son from a first marriage was murdered by her second husband and the son of her second marriage. In retribution she had the murderers killed. The legal problem is whether to treat her as a murderess. Pantagruel holds that it would have been appropriate to abandon any attempt to reason out the question, and resort instead to lottery:

> Qui eust decidé le cas au sort des dez, il n'eust erré, advint ce que pourroit. Si contre la femme, elle meritoit punition, veu qu'elle avoit faict la vengeance de soy, laquelle appartenoit à Justice. Si pour la femme, elle sembloit avoir eu cause de douleur atroce. (p. 511)

He presents these alternative verdicts as a dilemma so fraught that no court would decide. That seems surprising. The two questions arising are quite normal in a criminal case. Was the woman guilty of a crime? If so, what punishment did she deserve? From Pantagruel's own words, the woman had clearly committed a crime by killing without authority: 'elle avoit faict la vengeance [. . .] laquelle appartenoit à Justice'. The second issue, that of punishment, is complicated by the extenuating circumstances of 'douleur atroce'. But to treat the question as insoluble is an exaggeration: it is normal to adjust penalties according to circumstances; more pertinently still, Pantagruel himself suggests something analogous in advising the judges of Myrelingues to deal mercifully with Bridoye, because of his weaknesses (ch. 43, p. 505).

Pantagruel's rather forced statement of the problem suggests radical pessimism about the *perplexité* due to legal difficulties. Similar concerns appear in Epistemon's reference to the possible conflicts between laws, 'les antinomies et contrarietez des loix, des edictz, des coustumes et ordonnances' (ch. 44, p. 513). Clearly, the heroes have deep misgivings about men's ability to administer justice, even when they are most earnestly trying to do so.

Finally, there is a parallel between the *perplexité* that the ablest may experience in the legal sphere and the 'perplexité d'esprit' of Panurge over his marriage (ch. 24, p. 311). In other words, the legal chapters are linked with the theme of the quest for enlightenment. The link helps confirm that Panurge is baffled, not merely because he is foolish – though it is a factor – but because he is human.

Chapters 49-52 recount the wondrous properties of *pantagruelion*. Scholars agree that they are based on Pliny's account of flax, which he more or less confused with hemp and asbestos (*1*, p. 552, n. 8; *9*, pp. 286-87). To modern readers, many claims in these pages seem fanciful, e.g. the alleged effect of garlic on magnets (ch. 51, p. 569). In one case the narrator himself expresses disbelief: of a reportedly fireproof tree, he says, 'Cherchez qui le croye; je m'en excuse' (ch. 52, p. 587). However, he claims that his own assertions are true, in his 'tant veritable histoire' (ch. 51, p. 569), especially those about *pantagruelion*:

> Ce que je vous ay dict est grand et admirable; mais, si vouliez vous hazarder de croire quelque aultre divinité de ce sacre Pantagruelion, je la vous dirois. Croyez la ou non, ce

m'est tout un. Me suffist vous avoir dict vérité. Vérité vous
diray. (ch. 52, p. 581)

But his attitude is off-hand: 'ce m'est tout un'. In such a context,
his assertions of veracity must be mocking. This allows him to
offer us a mixture of serious and facetious material, and leave us
to puzzle about which is which.

One thing which these chapters certainly suggest is real awe
at nature's marvels, as in this example of a plant owing its name
to its wondrous properties:

heliotrope, c'est soulcil, qui suyt le soleil, car, le soleil le-
vant, il s'espanouist; montant, il monte, declinant, il decline,
soy cachant, il se cloust . . . (ch. 50, p. 565)

Human skill is also praised. The next chapter extols products
of hemp, such as sacking, rope and sail-cloth (ch. 51, pp. 575-
79). This is partly facetious; after the earlier satire on lawyers, it
is ironic indeed for the narrator to laud the role of the plant in
carrying lawyers' papers, 'Sans elle, comment seroient portez les
playdoiers des advocatz à l'auditoire?' (p. 575). But we may take
more seriously much of the praise, such as that of sails and shipping, thanks to which,

sont les nations, que Nature sembloit tenir [. . .] incongneues,
à nous venues, nous à elles: choses que ne feroient les oy-
seaulx [. . .] quelque liberté de nager en l'aër que leur soit
baillée par Nature. (p. 577)

Though the facetious tone soon returns, with the suggestion that
Pantagruel's descendants might go even farther and attain divin-
ity for themselves (p. 579), the triumphs of human art over
Nature are plainly celebrated here.

Finally, this section contains more praise of Pantagruel. One
reason given for the plant's name is

ses vertus et singularitez; car, comme Pantagruel a esté l'idée
et exemplaire de toute joyeuse perfection [. . .] aussi en Pantagruelion je recognoys tant de vertus [. . .] (ch. 51, p. 573)

The parallel between the preeminent qualities of Pantagruel and of *pantagruelion* suggests that praise of the plant is also indirect praise of the character. The work closes, as it began, with affirmation of Pantagruel's standing.

Despite its lack of plot and apparently random sequence of episodes, the *Tiers Livre* centres fairly coherently round the leading themes of *pantagruelisme* and enlightenment. The characters, too, are a coherent group in that Panurge is a foil to Pantagruel and his like-minded associates. The work is markedly ethical: enlightenment has often to do with problems of leading life aright; and judgment is a major element within *pantagruelisme*. Of course 'ethical' does not mean 'moralistic'; the *Tiers Livre* is certainly not that. The work gives an evenly balanced view of mankind. Panurge's quest amply exhibits human folly and, with the Bridoye episode, the weaknesses of human understanding. The satirical passages give full weight to men's evil. On the other hand, the ideal wisdom of *pantagruelisme* and the creations celebrated in the closing chapters show more positively what men can aspire to, and what they can do.

Finally, though it is made clear that the religious dimension has overriding significance, the book mostly concerns the problems of this life. The perspective changes in the *Quart Livre*.

3

The Quart Livre (1552)

A partial version of the *Quart Livre* appeared in 1548, a revised and completed version in 1552 (*3*, pp. vii-xviii). Here I consider only the 1552 version.

The *Quart Livre* narrates part of the journey to consult the Dive Bouteille about Panurge's prospects in marriage, and is thus an ostensible continuation of the *Tiers*. In reality, however, the *Quart* does not centre on Panurge, and hardly mentions marriage, save perhaps in chapter 9 (see *24*). The *Quart* is simply an account of episodes occurring as the voyagers sail from island to island.

The Prologue introduces major themes, *mediocrité* ('moderation') and faith. Chapters 1-4 stress the travellers' dependence on divine providence. The Dindenault episode (chs 5-8) is partly about greed, i.e., lack of moderation; chapters 9-11 focus on food and thence on gluttony. Chapters 12-16, on the Chiquanoux, satirize vexatious litigants and the wrongs of local justices (see p. 63, below, and *28*).

Chapter 17, enumerating strange deaths, foreshadows the mortal perils of the following episodes. Chapters 18-32, the core of the work, deal with religious themes. The storm (chs 18-24) is an occasion for discussing faith, Providence and human activity; allegorically, this section also raises the question of salvation. Chapters 25-28 reflect on the deaths of heroes, including Christ, and contain explicit reference to salvation; in contrast, chapters 29-32 deal with a perverse approach to salvation, particularly through fasting.

Exotic encounters follow: with the whale (chs 33-34), the Andouilles (chs 35-42), and the island of Ruach (chs 43-44). The Andouilles episode is partly religious satire, again touching on salvation through fasting. Ruach, whose inhabitants live on air, takes up the theme of moderation and excess, exemplifying the opposite extreme to the later episode of the Gastrolastres.

The section on Papefiguiere and Papimanie (chs 45-54) is religious satire, chiefly against the alleged role of the papacy in granting salvation. Chapters 55-56 (the 'parolles gelées') include, amongst other things, a praise of silence which contrasts with aspects of Papimanie.

Food is the focus of chapters 57-65, first with Gaster and the Gastrolastres (chs 57-62), then in the voyagers' meal (chs 63-65). This section relates to the theme of moderation (and greed), and to religious matters, particularly fasting. Finally, chapters 66-67 highlight Panurge's cowardice.

This rough outline should at least indicate that certain themes weave through the book and give a degree of cohesion. Otherwise, the work is held together by the presence of the same group of characters, each behaving in a consistent way. These two factors are crucial, because there is no plot, and the *Quart* lacks the unity which Panurge's concern with marriage imparts to the *Tiers*.

Before we turn to content, two structural features need further comment. The first is the seemingly inconclusive endings of some episodes: the voyagers simply depart, offering neither explicit opinions on what they have witnessed, nor remarks which would link the episode with others. (See, for example, the ends of chapters 16, 44, 47, 54, 56.) These non-committal endings reflect the praise of silence, to which I shall turn later. (Obviously, some of the apparently inconclusive episodes may well embody firm implied judgments.)

The second feature is the ending of the book, which stops in mid-voyage, for no clear intrinsic reason. Commentators have sought to account for or ascribe meaning to this arbitrary close (e.g., *23*, pp. 181-206). However, as the *Quart Livre* is not built round a plot or the guiding question of Panurge's marriage, the reader has no reason to expect a conclusive ending, and the lack of one seems no deficiency. Moreover, the prominence of Panurge's cowardice links chapters 66-67 adequately with earlier episodes (e.g., chs 18-24, 33-34, 55-56) and so rounds off the work. I do not, therefore, think it necessary to try to account for the abrupt ending.

We may begin our study of content by tracing some religious themes from the Prologue: *mediocrité*, faith, and Providence. We shall then look at the question of salvation, which is already bound up with faith and with Providence. This leads on to religious satire, which mainly concerns perverse approaches to salvation. We next consider *pantagruelisme*, and then the Gaster episode, which has implications for the status of mankind. Finally, we shall consider some characters in the *Quart Livre.*

A leading theme of the Prologue is *mediocrité*, which is 'precieuse, de tous louée, en tous endroictz agréable' (p. 14). As *mediocrité* is good in all fields, the term's connotations may vary according to context. (Thus, the translation 'moderation' is not always apt.) The Prologue connects *mediocrité* with religion, declaring it pleasing to God: 'de ceulx les prieres n'ont jamais esté esconduites qui ont mediocrité requis' (p. 14). The text gives two examples based loosely on the Bible. Zaccheus, being too short to see Christ in a crowd, 'soubhaitoit, rien plus, veoir nostre benoist Servateur [. . .] C'estoit chose mediocre et exposée à un chascun' (ib.). Here, *mediocrité* is to seek for oneself only what is available in normal circumstances to a normal person. The second case concerns the lost axe-head miraculously retrieved from the Jordan by the prophet Elisha (II Kings VI.1-7). The narrator muses, 'S'il eust soubhaité monter es cieulx dedans un charriot flamboiant comme Helie [. . .] l'eust-il impetré? C'est une question' (p. 15). The question seems to invite a negative answer. This case confirms the first, and adds implicitly that it would not be excessive to pray for a miracle to achieve an end that is itself *mediocre*, such as recovering an axe-head. The associated examples of excess also confirm that *mediocrité* and excess are two facets of the same theme. These two biblical examples illuminate the Prologue's first mention of *mediocrité*, which concerns health. The essential point is thus not that moderation is healthy, but a religious consideration: 'le vouloir du tresbon, tresgrand Dieu' is that all men be healthy (p. 12); thus, to seek and pray for good health is *mediocre*.

The later occurrences of the theme in the Prologue involve excesses in seeking wealth. The 'perdeurs de coingnées', who expect Jupiter to replace with golden axes the ordinary ones that they have 'lost' on purpose, are an amusing example of greed's leading to a bad end (p. 27). More meaningful are those who wonder why God will not enrich them immeasurably, 'car il est tout puissant. Un million d'or luy est aussi peu qu'un obole'. The narrator retorts, 'Paix: st, st, st; humiliez vous davant sa sacrée face et recongnoissez vos imperfections' (p. 28). Seeking exorbitant wealth, the very opposite of *mediocrité*, can lead to reprehensible questioning of Providence. Conversely, *mediocrité* in religion entails acceptance of one's lot, and submission to the will of God.

The theme of *mediocrité* and excess also concerns eating and drinking. At one extreme are the voracious Gastrolastres (chs 58-60), at the other the natives of Ruach, who live on air (chs 43-44). For both, inactive consumption is an end in itself. The narrator condemns the Gastrolastres as 'tous ocieux [. . .] charge inutile de la Terre' (ch. 58, p. 213). Criticism of Ruach lurks in Pantagruel's insidious praise:

> Si repcevez l'opinion de Epicurus, disant le bien souverain consister en volupté (volupté, diz je, facile et non penible), je vous repute bien heureux. Car vostre vivre, qui est de vent, ne vous couste rien, ou bien peu: il ne fault que souffler. (44, p. 168)

Associating the islanders' diet with the name of Epicurus may be pejorative. (On contemporary opinion about Epicurus, see *20*.) Certainly, it is implied that they are idle. Likewise, Hypene-mien's lamentations reveal that they are almost impotent against Bringuenarilles, who eats their windmills (p. 169), or the vaga-ries of passing showers, which calm the breezes: 'Ainsi sont maints repas perduz par faulte de victuailles' (p. 168). In their inertia, the islanders seem little preferable to the Gastrolastres.

The heroes' meal off Chaneph, though huge (ch. 64, p. 236), avoids such defects. The distinction concerns less the amount consumed than the characters' attitude. They feast for pleasure, indeed, but also to satisfy need, and with due gratitude to the Creator, 'qui par ce bon pain [. . .] nous guerist de telles pertur-bations tant du corps comme de l'ame' (ch. 65, p. 239). Symbol-ically, as they feast, a breeze rises and the previously becalmed ship resumes its voyage. Consumption here is neither mere indulgence nor an end in itself, but an agreeable prelude to activity. Even in the mundane area of eating and drinking, *mediocrité* and excess readily reflect the work's wider religious and moral values.

In the Prologue, the narrator refers several times to faith. Encouraging his readers to pray for health, he says, 'J'ay cestuy espoir en Dieu qu'il oyra nos prieres, veue la ferme foy en laquelle nous les faisons' (p. 14). In the story of the axe-head, Elisha 'pria Dieu le luy vouloir rendre [. . .] Et en ferme foy et confiance jecta [. . .] le manche après la coingnée' (p. 15). Linking 'ferme foy' with 'espoir en Dieu' and 'confiance', these cases stress that faith is a matter of trust in God. Like Pantagruel's 'confiance en la commiseration et ayde de nostre Seigneur' (ch. 4, p. 45), they anticipate key episodes.

The main one is the death of Pan (ch. 28). Pantagruel tells that, in antiquity, a report had circulated of weird voices bewailing the death of the great god Pan. Pantagruel interprets the voices as having lamented Christ's crucifixion. The interpretation rests partly on the name Pan, meaning 'all' in Greek: 'il [Christ] est le nostre Tout, tout ce que sommes, tout ce que vivons, tout ce que avons, tout ce que esperons est luy, en luy, de luy, par luy' (ch. 28, p. 124). Christ is thus the supreme object of faith. Pantagruel stresses two points. First, men depend for salvation on Christ alone, 'celluy grand Servateur des fidelles' (p. 124) and 'nostre unique Servateur' (p. 125). Secondly, he emphasizes the love of Christ, 'le grand pasteur, qui [. . .] non seulement a en amour et affection ses brebis, mais aussi ses bergiers' (p. 124). Pantagruel's attitude emerges both in his words and his demeanour: 'ce propous finy, resta en silence et profonde contemplation. Peu de temps après, nous veismes les larmes decouller de ses œilz grosses comme œufz de austruche' (p. 125). Nowhere else does Pantagruel shed tears. This unique passage shows that he feels towards Christ trust, faith, and also love. Here we see a difference in perspective between the *Tiers Livre* and the *Quart*: the *Tiers,* though undoubtedly Christian, does not mention Christ at all, while the *Quart* instals Him, quietly, at the centre of things.

A pervasive theme of the *Tiers Livre* is the primacy of God's will, both in His commands to men in general, and in His providential designs for each individual (e.g. chs 10, 30). In the *Quart* the theme recurs, sharply dramatized, during the storm which nearly shipwrecks Pantagruel (chs 18-24). Panurge excepted, the company strives by all human means to save the ship. In addition, Pantagruel prays for God's help, both as the storm comes on (ch. 19, p. 96) and also when, at its height, human resources can do no more: 'Seigneur Dieu, saulve nous; nous perissons. Non toutesfoys advieigne scelon nos affections ['wishes'], mais ta saincte volunté soit faicte' (ch. 21, p. 104). This prayer clearly embodies the trusting faith in God apparent in the Prologue and recalls the attitude of humble entreaty and submission commended by Pantagruel and Hippothadée in the *Tiers Livre*. But there is a change from the *Tiers*, in that Pantagruel is clearly afraid, not calmly residing in the 'deificque manoir de raison' (*TL*, ch. 2, p. 97); the *Quart Livre* is notably without such hints of god-like qualities in man. Also, the prayer partly echoes that of Christ Himself on the Mount of Olives (Luke XXII.42) or at Gethsemane (Matthew XXVI.39; Mark, XIV.36). The echo, which shows Pantagruel seeking to follow Christ's example, underlines the central role of Christ in the religious outlook of the *Quart Livre*. At the same time, because Pantagruel's fear recalls the humanity and sufferings of Christ, the episode foreshadows the pages on the death of Pan.

What of the travellers' own efforts to save themselves? Epistemon states their worth. He recognizes that the time and fashion of a man's death depend on God's will, and that men should therefore pray constantly for His mercy (ch. 23, pp. 109-10). But, he continues,

> là ne fault faire but et bourne: de nostre part, convient
> pareillement nous evertuer, et, comme dict le sainct Envoyé
> [St Paul], estre cooperateurs avecques luy [God]. (p. 110)

It is, then, God's will that men strive to help themselves. But the episode conveys that the outcome of their endeavours is strictly subject to His Providence. Having failed to control the ship, the crew lets it run before the wind, and the master's final order is, 'Chascun pense de son ame, et se mette en devotion, n'esperans ayde que par miracle des Cieulx!' (ch. 20, p. 101). Only after this does the storm abate, enabling the crew to regain control of the vessel (ch. 22, p. 105). The voyagers are thus shown as being saved by a providential change in the weather.

These chapters, while relating to men's earthly fates, may additionally refer to the hereafter. The ship seeking safe haven seems to be an allegory for the soul seeking salvation. Certainly, in the *Tiers Livre*, Pantagruel termed death 'port tresceur et salutaire, port de repous et de tranquilité' (*TL*, ch. 21, p. 281). Allegorically, the storm suggests that men must work for their own salvation – obviously by leading life according to God's will – but that it depends on Him whether they succeed.

Panurge's behaviour here differs sharply from his companions'. Terror-stricken, he 'restoit de cul [. . .] pleurant et lamentant' (ch. 19, p. 96), begging his shipmates to save him (e.g., ch. 20, p. 101). On the religious level, he suggests that all pay for someone to make a pilgrimage on their behalf – if they survive, presumably (ch. 20, p. 102). He implores the aid of the saints (e.g., ch. 18, p. 94) and makes a vow to St Michael, St Nicholas, and Christ:

> Je vous foys icy bon veu et à Nostre Seigneur que, si à ce coup m'estez aydans, j'entends que me mettez en terre hors ce dangier icy, je vous edifieray une belle grande petite chappelle ou deux. (ch. 19, p. 98)

Not content with all this, he also prays to God. In so far as the episode is about the earthly peril of shipwreck, Panurge clearly fails to help himself. By his persistent recourse to saints, he ignores the exclusive preeminence of the will of God. In bargaining for safety, as in his vow, he lacks the humility of Pantagruel, who simply beseeches God's mercy, and accepts His will. In so far as the episode concerns salvation, all the above points apply equally; we need add only that Panurge fails to recognize the unique position of Christ as Saviour. Panurge's conduct, then, is a foil to his companions' attitudes and behaviour.

A last cautionary word is needed on the treatment of Providence in the *Quart Livre*. We have seen the narrator rebuke those who wonder why God should not enrich them enormously (Prologue, p. 28). The point for present purposes is that, because Providence is impenetrable, and speculation about it presumptuous, the book cannot purport to unveil the subject; whatever hints the text may offer, and however it may advocate trust and faith, it must ultimately treat Providence as an unfathomable mystery. (Symptomatically, the *Quart Livre*, unlike the *Tiers*, says little of divination: the main discussions concern prophetic names [ch. 37], and portents that may foreshadow deaths of great men [chs 26-27].)

According to the *Tiers Livre*, Scripture shows men how to lead their lives. The emphasis on Scripture reappears in the *Quart*, though the perspective is different. Here, the admissions of a naïve devil testify to the importance of the Bible. His work includes finding souls for 'monsieur Lucifer' to devour. Various victims are still readily available, but he complains that students are no longer vulnerable:

> [Lucifer] se souloit ['used to'] desjeuner de escholiers. Mais (las!) ne sçay par quel malheur, depuys certaines années, ilz ont avecques leurs estudes adjoint les sainctz Bibles. Pour ceste cause plus n'en pouvons au Diable l'un tirer. (ch. 46, p. 176)

The roles of Scripture in leading men towards salvation and in laying down God's commands for the conduct of life are complementary. However, the stress placed here on salvation marks a new priority compared with the *Tiers Livre*, and reflects the same shift in interest which brings Christ as Saviour to the fore. By suggesting that students' interest in Scripture is new, the devil's words also recognize implicitly the impact of those advocating Bible-centred Christianity, i.e. Protestants, and also Catholic humanists, such as Lefèvre d'Étaples (ca 1450-1537), who had tried in various ways to reform and revitalize the Church from within. (These internal early reformers, who were often influenced by Erasmus, are sometimes called '*évangéliques*'. The term is handy, though it covers many shades of opinion.)

Moreover, our devil despairs of ever capturing student souls again, 'si les Caphards ['hypocrites'] ne nous y aident, leurs ous-tans par menaces, injures, force, violence et bruslements leur sainct Paul d'entre les mains' (ib.). The word 'caphard' is too general to designate specific oppressors, but the text certainly indicates that violent enforcement of Catholic orthodoxy, with its distrust of individual study of Scripture, does the work of the Devil by closing a way to salvation.

This passage occurs within the episode of the Papefigues and the Papimanes, the most important of several examples of religious satire, which are chiefly, though not wholly, about divergent views of salvation. The Papimanes are ardent devotees of the papacy who see the pope as 'Dieu en terre' (ch. 48, p. 180), and also await his coming as a Messiah (ch. 48, p. 182). Typically, they revere a portrait of the pope, exhibited only at major festivals (ch. 50, p. 186). Their devotion also includes the *Decretals*. Historically, these were collected rulings on points of doctrine or canon law by popes such as Gregory IX. To Homenaz, however, the *Decretals* are holy writ, and popes are not their authors but their propagators and protectors: a pope is 'evangeliste d'icelles et protecteur sempiternel' (ch. 49, p. 184); the term 'evangeliste' implicitly equates the *Decretals* with the Gospel. Furthermore, the Papimanes claim their own text is the original, and particularly holy for having descended ready written from Heaven (ib.).

If idolatry is the transfer to other beings of worship due to God, the Papimanes are idolaters and the three objects of their devotion (pope, portrait and *Decretals*) are their idols. Homenaz's own words confirm the point. He calls the *Decretals* (mere copies as well as the so-called 'original'), 'ces sacres livres, les quelz doibviez baiser et adorer, je diz d'adoration de latrie, ou de hyperdulie pour le moins' (ch. 52, p. 192). In Roman Catholic theology, 'dulie' was the veneration accorded to the saints, 'latrie' the worship reserved for God alone.

The Papimanes believe their idols enormously potent. Homenaz claims that, for an era of earthly bliss to ensue, it is necessary, but also sufficient, that men single-mindedly study and apply the *Decretals*: 'O lors et non plus toust, ne aultrement, heureux le monde!' (ch. 51, p. 190). Pending such general felicity, particular individuals who devote themselves to the *Decre-

tals can be 'dictz et reputez vrais Christians' (ch. 53, p. 197) and, by this reputation, gain temporal success, which, furthermore, will lead to salvation, dispensed by the pope:

> vous serez riches et honorez en ce monde. Je dis consequem-
> ment qu'en l'aultre vous serez infailliblement saulvez on
> benoist royaulme des Cieulx, du quel sont les clefz baillées à
> nostre bon Dieu Decretaliarche. (ch. 53, p. 200)

Such is the Papimanes' belief in the pope's power over salvation, that they think merely seeing his portrait brings forgiveness for many sins (ch. 50, p. 186). What is the source of his power? Illuminatingly, Homenaz prays to the pontiff, 'O mon bon Dieu [. . .] donne ordre que ces precieux œuvres de supererogation, ces beaulx pardons au besoing ne nous faillent' (ch. 53, p. 200). This alludes to the doctrine that the saints, in their earthly lives, had done works more meritorious than necessary to earn their own salvation ('supererogatory works'), and that their superfluous merit could be applied by the Church to save sinners who themselves lacked merit. Whatever the niceties of the doctrine, Homenaz understands it to mean that the pope has god-like power over the destinations of men's souls in the hereafter.

Historically, one of the channels whereby merit from supererogatory works was held to be applied to sinners was the indulgence or 'pardon'. In theory, such indulgences were to be granted only to the repentant. In practice, churchmen sometimes depicted them as automatically efficacious, whatever the sinner's spiritual state, and quite simply sold them to anyone willing to pay. As we have seen, Homenaz connects the obtaining of salvation from the pope with having worldly wealth (ch. 53, p. 200). And if the pope's power over salvation lies in his control of indulgences, then the hint is that salvation can simply be bought from him in that form. (As is well known, one of the most passionate complaints of Luther was against just this 'mechanical' view of indulgences, and the practice of selling them without question to anyone prepared to pay.)

Dread of damnation underlies the Papimanes' idolatry. For example, having prayed to the pope to save him from the 'gueule horrificque d'Enfer', Homenaz 'commença [. . .] jecter grosses et chauldes larmes, batre sa poictrine, et baiser ses poulces en croix' (ch. 53, p. 200). His feverish devotional gestures recall, discreditably, Panurge's craven performance during the storm. In each case, superstition and passivity accompany mind-numbing terror.

But the Papimanes are also ruthless to opponents of the papacy. Thus, Homenaz disgorges his hatred of all who resist the *Decretals*: 'Bruslez [. . .] carbonnadez ces meschans Hereticques Decretalifuges, Decretalicides, pires que homicides' (ch. 53, p. 197). A practical application of this outlook is the massacre of the Papefigues to avenge one individual's obscene gesture at the papal portrait (ch. 45, pp. 171-72). The text does not explicitly link the reprisals with the Papimanes' terror of damnation, but the link is easy to supply, since the Papimanes prize the picture for bringing forgiveness of sins. The Papimanes thus present a coherent amalgam of credulity, idolatry, and fanatical savagery.

The Papimanes' views are at odds with those advanced elsewhere by the heroes. For example, making the pope arbiter of men's salvation flouts the supremacy of God's will; the alleged role of supererogatory works conflicts with the idea that Christ is sole Saviour of men. Panurge praises the Papimanes for avoiding heresy, unlike England or Germany (ch. 50, p. 188). As his religious views have been shown wanting, praise from him amounts to oblique criticism by the text. Otherwise, the heroes' treatment of the Papimanes is more or less mocking. In his hosts' presence, Pantagruel says, 'oncques ne veiz Christians meilleurs que ces bons Papimanes' (ch. 54, p. 201). Beyond doubt, these words are ironic, and cannot mean that he thinks the Papimanes good Christians. Screech has shown that the expression 'bon christian' was used among Vatican courtiers to mean 'simpleton', and has suggested that this is the sense of the words 'meilleurs christians' here (*22*). One may easily agree that Pantagruel regards his hosts as morons, not least because he is merely giving a discreditable nuance to Homenaz's own words, 'Nous sommes simples gens' (ch. 54, p. 201). The imputation of naïvety is justified by the Papimanes' obvious credulity: for example, on the strength of Panurge's mere claim to have seen three popes, they

prostrate themselves (literally and figuratively) before the travellers (ch. 48, pp. 180-82). The irony against them would be
doubly pointed, granted a Roman source for 'meilleurs christians'.

Sometimes mockery lies in derisive asides, such as the response to Homenaz's tearful devotions:

> Epistemon, frere Jan et Panurge [. . .] commencerent, au cou-
> vert de leurs serviettes, crier: Myault, myault, myault, faig-
> nans ce pendent de s'essuer les œilz, comme s'ilz eussent
> ploré. (ch. 54, pp. 200-01)

Some mockery, particularly of the *Decretals* (ch. 52, *passim*), is
overt. Homenaz seems impervious to all this derision. At the end
of the banquet, he still calls his visitors 'amis', and distributes
gifts of 'grosses et belles poyres' (ch. 54, p. 201). That the
heroes have been able to toy with Homenaz indicates their supe-
riority over him. It shows similarly a capacity to laugh at the evil
embodied in the Papimanes. But these chapters do not suggest
that such evil can simply be laughed off. The slaughter of the
Papefigues rules out that reading.

The Papefigues were initially victims of the Papimanes, but
their suffering did not end with the massacre. Once rich, they are
now impoverished: 'tous les ans avoient gresle, tempeste, famine
et tout malheur, comme eterne punition de peché de leurs ances-
tres et parens' (ch. 45, p. 172). The young devil's words to the
peasant indicate that devils are the immediate cause of these
woes: 'depuys l'heure et le temps qu'au Pape vous feistes la
figue, tout ce pays nous feut adjugé, proscript et abandonné' (ch.
45, p. 173). Though the text leaves unspecified the source of the
curse under which the Papefigues appear to have fallen, one
point does arise clearly in connexion with the young devil and
his peasant victim. As we have seen, the devil admits that the
main way to rout devils is to follow Scripture. However, 'par le
conseil du curé' (ch. 47, p. 177), the peasant hides from his
adversary in a font of holy water, amid priests reciting formulae
of exorcism (ch. 45, p. 172). No-one pronounces on the worth of
such practices, but Pantagruel's question, 'quelz jeux c'estoient

qu'ilz jouoient là' (ib.), sounds sceptical. Moreover credit for beating the devil goes expressly to the peasant's wife: 'la vieille avoit trompé le Diable et guaingné le champ' (ch. 47, pp. 177-78). The juxtaposition makes the priests' measures against the devil seem futile.

These pages may reflect contemporary events. Some commentators see the fate of the Papefigues as an allusion to the Vaudois communities massacred on the Luberon in April 1545 by troops acting under the authority of the Parlement of Aix (*3*, p. 328; *9*, pp. 402-03). The Vaudois were religious dissenters with origins going back certainly to the fourteenth century, perhaps even to the twelfth. Some of their traditional beliefs, e.g. denial of purgatory, gave them affinity with the Reformers, and there were contacts with the latter in the 1530s (*17*, pt II and ch. 10). The massacre itself was part of the growing religious repression over which François Ier presided late in his reign (*19*, pp. 373-77). Being, for its day, an act of outstanding savagery, the slaughter of the Vaudois produced scandal and revulsion. Consequently, the Papefigues episode might well have reminded a contemporary reader of the Vaudois. However, the parallel can be taken no farther. Apart from the scale of the slaughter, the case of the Vaudois offers no obvious counterparts to major features of the Papefigues episode (e.g. the conditions for obtaining mercy or the inflammatory gesture at the papal portrait, ch. 45, pp. 171-72).

The chapters on the Papimanes may allude to a rift between the French Crown and Rome, known as the *crise gallicane* of 1551. This dispute between Henri II and Pope Julius III became so bitter that the King and his Council, at a meeting on 4 or 5 August 1551, considered setting up an independent Gallican (French) Church, not unlike Henry VIII's Church of England. The quarrel arose from political rivalry in Italy and from friction over the General Council of the Church (the Council of Trent). The Council had been meeting intermittently for years to consider, from a strictly orthodox point of view, the internal reform of the Catholic Church and its teachings. For what seem to have been largely political reasons, Henri threatened, at one point, to set up a separate Gallican Council to deal with problems in the

Catholic Church in France. To do so while the General Council was in being would have been a denial of its authority over the Catholic Church in France. The crisis in fact abated. By September 1551, Julius was seeking peace, and reconciliation was completed by April 1552.

In the Papimanes episode, the attack on the *Decretals* includes the fiscal claims of the papacy (ch. 53, p. 197) and the assertion of papal supremacy over kings (ch. 53, p. 199). On the first point, it is noteworthy that royal orders were in fact published on 3 September 1551 forbidding payment of any dues to the pope for the expedition of benefices in France. As to the second, Julius repeatedly threatened to depose and excommunicate Henri. Chapter 53 need not allude to precise events such as the royal orders of September 1551; what is more plausible is to say that the question of papal authority was conspicuously topical. It should also be said that the satire in these pages is directed less against the pope than his over-zealous supporters. (For more background information, see *21*, Bk 2, ch. 2.)

Another episode of religious satire, again involving salvation, is on Quaresmeprenant (chs 29-32). He personifies the privations of Lent, whence his enmity with the Andouilles (ch. 29, pp. 126-27), which were of course forbidden in Lent. Indulgences being a Lenten preoccupation, he is also 'foisonnant en pardons' (ch. 29, p. 126). The background to his strife with the Andouilles is partly literary. Allegorical battles between Lent and Carnival were a well-established subject for plays, such as *La dure et cruelle Bataille et paix du glorieux sainct Pensart à l'encontre de Caresme* of the 1480s (in *16*). However, the episode also involves sharp satirical thrusts. From a bizarre anatomical description of Quaresmeprenant, Pantagruel concludes that he is a monster (ch. 32, p. 135). This is condemnation, as emerges from the treatment later in the chapter of other monsters such as the children of Antiphysie.

One reason for hostility is that Lent is tainted with hypocrisy. Chapter 32 opens with a fanciful list of Quaresmeprenant's *contenences*, his physical and mental functions. When he spits artichokes and snores beans (p. 133), such emissions, though caricatural, are at least consistent with Lenten fare. But to weep duck and sigh smoked tongue are not, and he is thus presented as a humbug. (On the medical aspects of Quaresmeprenant, see *18*.)

More radical objections to fasting lurk, oddly, in the chapters on Gaster and the Gastrolastres. At its simplest, that section ridicules excess: the effigy Manduce with 'les œilz plus grands que le ventre' (ch. 59, p. 215) is an allegory of monstrous greed for food and drink. Worse, however, the Gastrolastres commit idolatry: 'Ilz tous tenoient Gaster pour leur grand Dieu [. . .] ne recongnoissoient aultre Dieu que luy' (ch. 58, p. 214). The link with fasting is that Gaster too has lean days (ch. 60). His dishes are meatless, but still nearly as many as usual, and quite enough for him to gorge himself: 'Ces viandes ['food'] devorées, s'il ne beuvoit, la Mort l'attendoit à deux pas près. L'on y pourvoyoit tresbien' (ch. 60, p. 222). Implicitly, if abstinence only means shunning meat, it is consistent with gluttony and 'worship' of the belly, and need not be Christian. Indeed, in spiritual terms, the advocates of Lenten abstinence are no better than the Gastrolastres, since all are equally preoccupied with the flesh. Such is the main underlying reason why Quaresmeprenant was earlier decried as a monstrosity.

The treatment of Quaresmeprenant may involve a specific gibe at the Council of Trent, which had lately reaffirmed the necessity of Lenten abstinence (*3*, pp. xxxii-xxxiii). This seems the simplest interpretation of the statement that the 'concile national de Chesil' had condemned the Andouilles (ch. 35, p. 144).

Has the *Quart Livre* a clear sectarian allegiance? The text gives one or two hints of sympathy with Protestants. One appears, as we have seen, when Panurge congratulates Homenaz on avoiding the heresies of England and Germany (ch. 50, p. 188). Elsewhere, the young devil, after deploring the influence of Scripture, confides that Lucifer has gone on a diet 'depuys qu'il eut sa forte colicque provenente à cause que es contrées Boréales l'on avoit ses [. . .] chaircuitiers oultragé villainement' (ch. 46, p. 176). The 'contrées Boréales' suggest the Protestant lands of northern Europe. The emphasis on Christ as sole Saviour and on the central importance of Scripture would be compatible with Protestantism; so would the symmetrically corresponding attacks on the cult of saints, on the doctrine of supererogatory works, on indulgences, Lent, and papal pretensions to control access to salvation. However, such views were also entertained by at least some *évangéliques*. As for the assault on papal claims to supremacy over princes, Protestants would have approved, but so would Henri II, who was in most respects conservatively Catholic.

It is also noteworthy that the Quaresmeprenant episode contains an attack on Calvin. The 'monsters' whom Pantagruel lambasts include 'les Demoniacles Calvins, imposteurs de Geneve' (ch. 32, p. 137). Coming from one so mild, this onslaught is arresting. There may be a biographical explanation, since Calvin had attacked Rabelais personally in his *Traité des Scandales* (1550). There are probably also theological reasons, centring on Calvin's doctrine of double predestination, i.e. that, irrevocably and from all eternity, some are predestined to be saved, others to be damned. When the narrator reproves speculation on 'la puissance et praedestination de Dieu' (Prologue, p. 28), the rebuke would presumably apply to Calvin. Moreover, his doctrine denies men any power to shape their own fates in the next life, and so conflicts with the views dramatized in the storm episode. True, Calvinism was not the only form of Protestantism, and an attack on Calvin is not an attack on all Protestantism. However, the worthlessness of men's works in earning salvation was a notoriously central feature of Luther's teaching as well as Calvin's, and our text does seem to diverge sharply from them on this point. Thus, while the text rejects much of traditional Catholicism and, of course, the repressive activities of the 'caphards', it is not Protestant. One could perhaps call it 'évangélique', though I doubt whether the term is precise enough to help much here.

What of *pantagruelisme* in this book? The *Tiers* stressed the generous tolerance of *pantagruelistes*. This quality reappears in the *Quart Livre*: e.g. Pantagruel is loath to believe the Andouilles treacherous (ch. 37, p. 152), and ready to forgive their attack (ch. 42, p. 164). However, it is less prominent than in the *Tiers*. Rather, the Prologue defines *pantagruelisme* as 'certaine gayeté d'esprit conficte en mespris des choses fortuites' (pp. 11-12). Here 'gayeté' is not mere merriment; the Pantagruel of the *Quart Livre* is himself grave, as he was in the *Tiers*. Linked with 'mespris des choses fortuites', this 'gayeté' is akin to the serenity already ascribed to Pantagruel in the earlier book. Greater emphasis on serenity here seems to cohere with the increased stress on Providence: 'gayeté', in this sense, and 'mespris des choses fortuites' befit the Christian who, like Pantagruel in the storm, believes himself ultimately in the hands of Providence.

Pantagruel's outlook has one major new feature, the promotion of silence or discretion. During the 'parolles gelées' episode, he tells Panurge, 'C'est acte de advocatz [. . .] vendre parolles. Je vous vendroys plus tost silence et plus cherement' (ch. 56, p. 207). The remark reflects the discretion which he shows elsewhere in the book. In some cases, he has strong views, but withholds them. For instance, when the Potestat d'Ennasin treats the voyagers as yokels, 'gens bottez de foin', he has a struggle to remain silent: 'le bon Pantagruel tout voyoit et escouttoit; mais à ces propous, il cuyda ['came near to'] perdre contenence' (ch. 9, p. 63). Another hint of retained views occurs when Pantagruel sees the 'beatz peres' sailing to the Council; he is silent, but also 'pensif et melancholicque', indicating 'fascherie non acoustumée' (ch. 18, p. 93).

Why promote discretion? Clearly, Pantagruel judges some discussions useless: he will not lecture hungry companions on hunger, since 'l'estomach affamé n'a poinct d'aureilles' (ch. 63, p. 233). But some discussion may be worse than useless. Priapus says the rival academics Ramus and Galland, 'allumoient [. . .] le feu de faction [. . .] entre les ocieux escholiers' (Prologue, p. 19), and he urges Jupiter to turn both to stone, 'A perpetuele memoire que ces petites philauties [. . .] plus tost davant vous contempnées feurent que condamnées' (pp. 19-20). Contentious debate can have bad consequences, factional strife, and spring from bad motives, self-love or *philautie*. Thus Pantagruel's discretion, e.g. over monastic gluttony (ch. 11, p. 68), seems inspired, at least partly, by fear of the inflammatory effects of debate. This may be connected in turn with growing awareness that words can mislead and arouse. The *Tiers Livre* helps put the matter in perspective. Talking of litigants, Epistemon deplores

la fraulde du Calumniateur infernal, lequel souvent se transfigure en messagier de lumiere par ses ministres, les pervers

advocatz [. . .] faict phantasticquement sembler à l'une et
l'aultre partie qu'elle a bon droict . . . (ch. 44, p. 513)

The warning is about lawyers' blandishments, but these seem
only a particular case of the devil's general power to spread conflict by the specious words of his agents. In the *Tiers Livre*,
Panurge wields the most obviously deceptive words, notably in
praising debtors and lenders (chs 3-4). In the *Quart* the most
nearly reminiscent passages are Homenaz's praise of the *Decretals* (chs 51, 53); both eulogies contain a vision of the Golden
Age, both plainly do not convince Pantagruel. But whereas
Panurge's speech is a fairly harmless conceit devised by a mere
châtelain, Homenaz accompanies his eulogy with exhortations
to crush and butcher opponents, and he has followers who do
those very things. No doubt the practical importance of his
rhetoric can be overstated; his guests seem little persuaded to
revere the *Decretals* or to kill anyone. Strikingly, however, the
explicit praise of silence comes in the very next episode. The hint
is that, though discerning listeners may be unimpressed, oratory
in the manner of Homenaz has the potential to mislead, inflame
feelings, and destroy. By the same token, we are reminded that
Homenaz is not just a buffoon, but also a tool of the 'Calumniateur infernal'. (On other readings of the 'parolles gelées', see *25*.)

It is Pantagruel's discretion which is highlighted. However,
the number of seemingly inconclusive episodes probably exemplifies the same tendency. (See above, p. 34.) The same may
apply to the changed role which the text gives to Panurge. In the
Tiers Livre, he shone by his inventive arguments and displays of
verbal fireworks; in the *Quart*, he is relatively subdued. It is as if
extremes of disputation had been moved from Pantagruel's circle
and from merely domestic matters, such as matrimony, to be
associated henceforth with religious fanatics and the bloody
horrors of the outside world.

We may now return to Gaster. As we have seen, this episode
condemns the Gastrolastres (and Quaresmeprenant). It implies
other things about mankind in general. Depicted as a tyrant,
Gaster is an allegory of men's enslavement to the need for food:
'Son mandement est nommé: faire le sault sans delay, ou mourir'

(ch. 57, p. 210). Though, as stated elsewhere, God provides for this need (ch. 65, p. 239), it can be anarchical to the point of cannibalism, as at the siege of Saguntum (ch. 57, p. 211). And yet the irresistible Gaster is, by his own admission, 'paouvre, vile, chetifve creature' (ch. 60, p. 223). The point of the paradox seems to be that men are ruled by a base appetite, and that from this angle they are indeed pitiful.

Gaster is also, according to the narrator, a master of invention: the account of his innovations occupies two chapters (chs 61-62). Some of his supposed inventions are of real things, e.g. carts (ch. 61, p. 224), others of imaginary devices, such as one to produce rain (ch. 61, p. 225). Some, medicine for instance, are plainly beneficent, but at least one, artillery, is described as devilish (ch. 61, p. 226). Their alleged common feature is that all arise from a need connected with grain: siege artillery, for example, is required to capture grain from others (ib.). Obviously, some, in reality, are not exclusively or even primarily linked with foodstuffs, e.g., cities (ch. 61, p. 225) or indeed artillery. Why credit Gaster with them? These chapters list some of men's most startling creations: shipping is 'chose de laquelle se sont les elemens esbahiz' (ib.); gunpowder a substance 'de laquelle Nature mesmes s'est esbahie, et s'est confessée vaincue par art' (ch. 61. p. 226). Some of these triumphs of art over nature, particularly shipping, recall the praise of *pantagruelion (TL*, chs 51-52). In the *Tiers Livre*, some of the praise is facetious, but much is genuine celebration of man's powers. However, the *Quart*, mixing destructive with beneficial inventions, conveys far less optimism about the use men make of their powers. Moreover, ascribing these inventions to Gaster stresses that man, for all his ingenuity, remains a frail and dependent being.

Gaster's devices to stop or repel missiles add another dimension. To prove the devices credible, he lists allegedly similar effects reported by ancient authorities:

> Le cas ne trouvoit difficile; attendu que l'herbe nommée *Aethiopis* ouvre toutes les serrures qu'on luy praesente, et que Echineis, poisson tant imbecille ['weak'], arreste [. . .] les plus fortes navires. (ch. 62, p. 228)

Almost throughout, Gaster alone rehearses these wonders, and the narrator makes no comment. Gaster's last example is:

> le suzeau croist, plus canore ['resonant'] et plus apte au jeu des flustes, en pays on quel le chant des coqs ne sera ouy [. . .] comme si le chant des coqs hebetast [. . .] la matiere et le boys du suzeau. (ch. 62, p. 230)

Thus far the case resembles most of the others. A normal effect, music from flutes of elder, is allegedly inhibited by another natural phenomenon, cocks crowing. But here the narrator does intervene to record possible allegorical interpretations:

> en ceste sentence nous enseignent que les gens saiges et studieux ne se doibvent adonner à la musicque triviale et vulgaire, mais à la celeste, divine, angelique, plus absconse et de plus loing apportée: sçavoir est d'une region en laquelle n'est ouy des coqs le chant. (ib.)

The references to two kinds of music themselves seem to be allegorical: the sage is urged to turn his mind from the earthly to the divine. The contemplation advocated is presumably the sort which is available to the wise man leading his life in the world, and which involves keeping the earthly and the divine in perspective, as exemplified by Pantagruel in both books. But this passage has a unique force, which lies in its conjunction with Gaster. The allegorical interpretation is what distinguishes it from Gaster's earlier examples: if they are even true, they stay on the level of material phenomena, Gaster's level; this last example, understood allegorically, 'plus haultement' (p. 230), escapes from the material level. The implication is that, despite Gaster's crushing rule over humanity, the wise may yet rise in spirit above their subjection.

Before we leave the *Quart Livre*, a few words about characters are needed. While Panurge is less conspicuous than in the *Tiers*, Frere Jean is more so. He not only intervenes quite often by word or action, but also gives a lead in several episodes (e.g. the Andouilles). The character remains schematic. He is violent,

as when he tests the willingness of the Chiquanoux to be beaten
for money (ch. 16, p. 86). He has strong appetites for food and
drink (e.g. ch. 10), and for sex (e.g. ch. 54, pp. 201-02). In the
former, at least, he is depicted as a typical monk, himself asking,
'Que signifie [. . .] que tousjours vous trouvez moines en
cuysines?' (ch. 11, p. 68). He is irreverent, blaspheming through
the storm (chs 19-22), and quoting the beggars who call a gan-
grenous leg a 'jambe de Dieu'. Pantagruel condemns this
expression in terms which suggest that irreverence, too, is typically monastic: 'User ainsi du sacre nom de Dieu en choses tant
hordes ['foul'] et abhominables! [. . .] Si dedans vostre moynerie
est tel abus de parolles en usaige, laissez le là' (ch. 50, p. 187).
By some of his faults, then, he is a medium for anti-monastic
satire.

He also has virtues. He is the very embodiment of activity
and self-help, particularly in trying to save the ship during the
storm. He is phenomenally brave, but capable of alarm, as at the
height of the tempest: 'Que tous les Diables de coup de mer
voicy! Nous n'eschappons jamais, ou je me donne à tous les Diables' (ch. 21, p. 104). Clearly, his daring is not mere stupidity,
and escapes Pantagruel's stricture that 'ne craindre, quand le cas
est evidentement redoutable, est signe de peu ou faulte de apprehension ['understanding']' (ch. 22, p. 108). Also, in religion, he
knows and follows his breviary, as far as it goes. Thus, of the im-
mortality of demi-gods, he says to Pantagruel, 'Cela [. . .] n'est
point matiere de breviaire. Je n'en croy si non ce que vous
plaira' (ch. 27, p. 122). By implication, if his breviary had said
anything on the subject, he would have felt constrained to
believe accordingly. In a work which emphasizes the authority
of Scripture, Frere Jean's creed seems dubious, though it is
obviously free from excesses such as those of the Papimanes.
Even here, however, there is something to commend, for, to the
extent that he adheres steadily to his creed, Frere Jean at least
shows some sense of religious principle.

Finally, there is his attitude to Panurge, to whom he is a pen-
dant by his courage and activity. He treats Panurge with a mixture of contempt and affection. While he reviles Panurge during
the storm, he is ready to protect him from Dindenault (ch. 5, p.

49), and they are clearly accomplices, for example, in mocking Homenaz (ch. 54, pp. 200-01).

As for Panurge, having already seen his part in the religious themes of the book, we need add only a few remarks. Physical cowardice, incipient in the *Tiers Livre*, becomes his dominant trait in the *Quart* (e.g. ch. 5, p. 49; chs 18-22, *passim*; ch. 29, p. 127; ch. 33, pp. 138-39; ch. 66, pp. 242-43; ch. 67, pp. 244-45, 247-48). The reason is plain. As his travels expose him to physical danger, fear of the latter naturally supplants the fear of cuckoldry which haunted him in the *Tiers*. The shift in focus marks no deep change in the character. Panurge's cowardice inspires some comic boasting, as when he assures his companions, '[je] ne crains rien, que les dangiers' (ch. 23, p. 111). This is a stock joke, recalling another literary character, the Franc Archer de Bagnolet, whose cowardice had become proverbial. Panurge himself makes the connexion later, on hearing strange voices at sea:

> Fuyons! Je n'ay poinct de couraige sus mer. En cave et ailleurs j'en ay tant et plus. Fuyons! Saulvons nous! je ne le diz pour paour que je aye, car je ne crains rien fors les dangiers. Je le diz tousjours. Aussi disoit le France archier de Baignolet. (ch. 55, p. 204)

In likening himself to the Franc Archer, Panurge admits to cowardice, but the comic associations of that character make a joke of it. Admissions of fear are not new in Panurge, but such humorous self-deprecation is unusual and engaging.

The drowning of Dindenault and his shepherds shows an aspect of Panurge not seen in the *Tiers Livre*. The episode is in two parts, an initial brush between the antagonists (ch. 5), then the fatal bargaining (chs 6-8). Dindenault begins by mocking Panurge and, when Panurge answers in kind, makes an apparently serious attempt to kill him (ch. 5, p. 49). Order is restored, and the two drink together as a 'signe de perfaicte reconciliation' (ib.). But Panurge still plans mischief: 'dist secretement à Epistemon et à frere Jan: "Retirez vous icy un peu à l'escart et joyeusement passez temps à ce que voirez"' (ch. 6, p. 49). At first, he may not mean to kill men, only sheep. In the end, however, his intentions are clearly homicidal, since he stops his human victims from climbing back on board (ch. 8, p. 57). His ploy is meant for amusement ('joyeusement') but also for revenge. He brags, 'Jamais homme ne me feist desplaisir sans repentence' (ch. 8, p. 58). Certainly, because he tried to kill Panurge, Dindenault may deserve retribution; but, as in the case of the woman of Smyrna (*TL*, ch. 44), Panurge has no right to exact it. As for the shepherds, they are guilty only of sharing Dindenault's mirth at Panurge's appearance (ch. 5, p. 48). Frere Jean alone comments on Panurge's behaviour. Asked by Panurge, 'Que t'en semble', he replies, 'Tout bien de vous', and complains only that Panurge has wasted money (ch. 8, p. 58). The phrase 'Tout bien de vous' suggests that his approval stems, partly at least, from personal loyalty. However, comradeship does not override all else. When Panurge vaunts his vengeance, Frere Jean adds a comment, which closes the episode: 'Tu [. . .] te damne comme un vieil diable. Il est escript: *Mihi vindictam, et caetera* Matiere de breviaire' (ch. 8, p. 58). As the pauline reference shows (Romans XII.19), Christianity rejects revenge; even Frere Jean's monkish religion, narrowly based on his breviary, cannot condone it. Panurge's conduct is thus duly condemned, but the fact that Frere Jean is a minor character allows the condemnation to be passed over lightly, and the whole episode to be left, as it were, in parenthesis.

The brutality of the episode is further mitigated because the text links it particularly with the theme of *mediocrité* and excess. Panurge complains that Dindenault's price for his sheep is too high, and adds significantly:

> Vous n'estes le premier de ma congnoissance qui, trop toust voulent riche devenir et parvenir, est à l'envers tombé en paouvreté, voire quelque foys s'est rompu le coul. (ch. 7, p. 55)

Dindenault's fate thus recalls that of the 'perdeurs de coingnées' who were dispatched in the Prologue, at the behest of a burlesque Jupiter, for their greed and dishonesty. As in that case, this is not a serious suggestion that the greedy deserve death, but a comically exaggerated cautionary tale indicating that excess leads to a fall.

The impression of cruelty is also attentuated as a consequence of the aside in which Panurge alerts Epistemon and Frere Jean that he has a ploy in mind (ch. 6, pp. 49-50). We naturally look forward with curiosity to the working out of his scheme and, because this curiosity can most readily be satisfied if it succeeds, curiosity turns readily into sympathy with the schemer and reluctance to blame his cruelty. Conversely, it makes it easy for us to accept his view of events, in the moments when he treats the ploy less as revenge than as a diversion. Thus, while we cannot wholly overlook the cruel, vengeful side of Panurge which briefly appears here, we tend to focus on the practical joker who airily dismisses the money squandered, 'c'est [. . .] bien chié pour l'argent! Vertus Dieu, j'ay eu du passetemps pour plus de cinquante mille francs' (ch. 8, p. 58). It is hard to feel repelled by such a character. (The Panurge whom we glimpse here of course recalls his earlier incarnation in *Pantagruel*, where he is often merely amusing, but sometimes vicious, e.g. in tormenting the 'haulte dame de Paris' [ch. 22].)

The *Quart Livre* proves, then, more coherent than might appear at first. For example, concern with salvation knits together several of the positive religious themes and much of the religious satire; Pantagruel's distaste for contention and his praise of silence cohere with a sense of the bloody horrors – however comically presented – of public affairs. The *Tiers Livre* evinces a sense of perspective taking in both this world and the next. So does the *Quart*, but it also gives an impression of turning away from this world. Possible examples are the two sections on human invention: the pages on Gaster show mankind less positively than those on *pantagruelion*; and while the *Tiers* associated the plant closely with Pantagruel, and praised him by praising it, the *Quart* would detach the wise man, such as Pantagruel, from the material world over which Gaster presides. The focus of the book's religious concerns on salvation is part of the same trend. Taking each book as a whole, these are simply changes of emphasis, but they are sustained enough to give the *Quart Livre*, unlike the *Tiers*, hauntingly valedictory tones.

4

The Ve Livre

MODERN editions of the posthumous *Ve Livre* are based on the three extant early versions, two printed, one manuscript. (Unless specified otherwise, I number chapters as in *4*.) The first version, entitled *L'Isle sonante,* bears the date 1562; it has 16 chapters and no Prologue; chapter 16 is about the Isle des Apedeftes (ch. 16, pp. 333-40 in *4*). A second version, entitled *Cinquiesme Livre* and dated 1564, comprises the Prologue, chapters 1-15 of the *Isle sonante*, a new chapter 16, *Comment nous passasmes Outre*, replacing the Apedeftes, and 32 further chapters. (In *4*, the chapter on Outre, pp. 340-42, is also numbered 16.) Finally, the manuscript version, probably a late sixteenth-century copy, resembles the *Cinquiesme Livre*; however, it lacks part of the Prologue and two whole chapters (chs 23-24 in *4*), and has one new chapter (ch. 32 *bis* in *4*). In addition to such large-scale discrepancies, the three texts often diverge in detail. For instance, one passage variously calls the same character: 'Frere Jehan des Enlumineures' (*Isle sonante*); 'frère Jean' (*Cinquiesme Livre*); and 'frère Jehan des Antonneures' (manuscript) (*VL*, ch. 12, p. 322, n. 4). (On the foregoing, see also *4*, II, pp. 263-64, 268-69.)

The authenticity of the *Ve Livre* has been denied by many scholars, and defended by many others. A frequent approach on both sides has been to consider the content and quality of the *Ve Livre*, compare them with the same aspects of earlier books by Rabelais, and thence conclude that the *Ve Livre* must be – or could not possibly be – by Rabelais. Interpretation of content being subjective, and appreciation of literary quality even more so, the debate has often been an inconclusive exchange of personal impressions. However, three studies seem particularly significant. The first, by A. Glauser (*26*), crystallizes the case against the work's authenticity. The summary below draws heavily on it.

Some arguments against authenticity relate to external circumstances. For example, Rabelais is unlikely to have had time to write the book, between publishing the definitive version of the *Quart Livre* (February 1552) and dying in April 1553 (*26*, p. 44). The delay of nine years before the *Isle sonante* appeared in 1562 makes it unlikely that this version was based on Rabelais's own papers (*26*, p. 48). The chapters unveiled two years later in the *Cinquiesme Livre* are similarly suspect (*26*, p. 49).

As for internal evidence, the text contains an allusion to Scaliger's *adversus Cardanum* published in 1557, after Rabelais's death (*VL*, ch. 18, p. 348 and n. 1). The text also has many echoes of material in previously published works by Rabelais: for example, the Prologue contains reminiscences of earlier prologues (*26,* pp. 76-78); the opening of chapter 1 echoes those of *Quart Livre* chs 2 and 5 (*26*, p. 84); the Fredons' Sunday diet 'provient certainement des listes d'"offrandes" des Gastrolâtres' (*26*, p. 156). Glauser argues that Rabelais could not conceivably have returned to this material so soon after the *Quart Livre* and thence that he did not in fact write the *Ve Livre*. According to Glauser, the echoes betray plagiarism. Even recurring subjects may be suspect: 'Un plagiaire voudra [. . .] s'astreindre à imiter les sujets de l'auteur authentique [. . .] La ressemblance des thèmes peut être un indice indéniable de fausseté: pourquoi en effet reprendre au *Ve Livre* des sujets parents du *Quart Livre* – comme la première partie de l'*Isle sonante* qui rappelle l'épisode des Papimanes?' (*26*, pp. 33-34).

Aesthetic arguments are also advanced. For Glauser, the *Ve Livre* so lacks Rabelais's qualities that it cannot be by Rabelais. For instance, he maintains that the characters have lost substance: 'Pantagruel perd de sa grandeur, Panurge de sa malice et de sa cruauté, Frère Jan de sa vivacité et de son esprit' (*26*, p. 114).

On the other side, Mme Huchon has argued for the book's partial authenticity (*27*). In her view, all material in the work is by Rabelais, save the Apedeftes chapter and a list at the beginning of chapter 32 *bis* (*27*, p. 488). However, the genuine material consists of drafts, written at different times, for more or less isolated episodes, and later assembled by various editors: 'Les éditeurs n'ont pas voulu abuser le public en lui présentant un livre qui ne serait pas de l'auteur; ils l'ont néanmoins fait en faisant prendre pour un Ve livre ce qui n'était que des brouillons

de livres antérieurs ou des notes de lecture' (ib.). Rabelais never
envisaged these drafts as a single work: 'le Ve livre n'a jamais
existé en tant que tel dans l'esprit de l'auteur' (*27*, p. 489).

Mme Huchon's belief in the genuineness of the drafts rests
on the fact that Rabelais's certainly authentic works exhibit a
unique spelling system and a characteristic use of negative particles. An example of the former is the distinctive ending -*ent*
which he gives to certain present participles; normally the verbs
concerned are derived from Latin verbs with present participles
ending in -*ens* (*27*, p. 243). As for negation, one example may
again serve. In Rabelais's other books, the particle *pas* is used
relatively little, and mainly with verbs of movement. In orthogra-
phy and negations, all three versions of the *Ve Livre* follow
Rabelais's practices enough to suggest that the material is his.
Conversely, the use of *pas* in the Apedeftes chapter does not
conform, whence Mme Huchon's conclusion that it is spurious
(*27*, pp. 462-63).

If she is right, some of the objections put by Glauser and
others seem to be met. The *Ve Livre* echoes other books, not
because it is derived from them, but because it includes drafts
prior to or roughly contemporary with them. The aesthetic short-
comings of the *Ve Livre* are to be expected in rough drafts, however great the writer. Mme Huchon also offers explanations for
at least some of the disparities between the early versions of
the work. Study of the variants invites the conclusions that all
three derive from the same draft material, and that the difficulty
of reading Rabelais's handwriting accounts for many divergences
in wording (*27*, pp. 435-39). Also, Mme Huchon thinks it unlikely that he had arranged in order the drafts underlying the
later chapters (17-47). The editors therefore used their discretion
in ordering material. They proceeded similarly in making omis-
sions, e.g. chapters 23 and 24, which were left out of the
manuscript (*27*, pp. 448-50).

Mme Huchon's work is persuasive, because it is extremely
thorough, and because it rests on objectively verifiable features
of the texts, not on readers' subjective impressions. Her conclusions are supported by another non-impressionistic inquiry, a
statistical study by G. A. Petrossian (*29*).

If we accept that the *Ve Livre* is basically a collection of Rabelais's drafts, there are still two obvious reasons for using the material with caution. First, there is the allusion to Scaliger's *adversus Cardanum*. Some have suggested that Rabelais might have known of the work by hearsay, or seen it in manuscript (*27*, p. 416, n. 17). However, interpolation seems at least as likely an explanation; and if there is one possible interpolation, there may well be others. The second reason for caution is even more obvious: the differences between the early versions of the *Ve Livre* mean that the texts which we now have are only an approximation to what Rabelais wrote.

As constituted in Jourda's edition, the *Ve Livre* has the following main sections. Chapters 1-8, describing the Isle sonante, satirize the monastic orders, and also the papacy. Chapters 11-15 revile the Chatz fourrez, i.e. the judiciary and legal profession. Chapters 17-24 are a jocular treatment of alchemy. Chapters 26-28 on the Freres Fredons attack monasticism and Lent. Chapters 29-30, on the Pays de Satin, describe a tapestry and embody sceptical views about certain ancient authors and modern geographical writers. The final section (chs 31-47) covers the consultation of the Dive Bouteille; the Bottle utters one word 'Trinch' ('drink') (ch. 44, p. 452), which is glossed to mean 'soyez vous mesmes interpretes de vostre entreprinse' (ch. 45, p. 454). In other words, Panurge is again told to make up his own mind.

The *Ve Livre* gives hints of ideas which Rabelais entertained, but did not publish. Its main value is as evidence about the *Tiers* and *Quart Livre*. This area is large and relatively unexplored; the following are merely examples of possible lines of inquiry. In some cases, the *Ve Livre* may help elucidate passages in those books. In other cases, comparing published and unpublished material may highlight peculiarities of tone and emphasis in the former. Finally, such comparisons may offer hints about Rabelais's aesthetic tendencies.

First, an example of elucidation. The *Tiers* and *Quart Livre* contain lists of marvellous natural phenomena reported by ancient writers: e.g., *TL*, ch. 51, pp. 569, 573-75; *QL*, ch. 62, pp. 228-30. It is sometimes unclear how seriously these wonders are offered for our acceptance. There may be some help in the *pays de Satin* (*VL*, chs 29-30), possibly written by 1545, before publication of the *Tiers Livre* (*27*, p. 485). These pages describe a 'pays de tapisserie' (ch. 30, p. 398). The marvels depicted include the remora, which Pliny claimed could halt a sailing-ship. The narrator states:

> J'y vy une Remore [. . .] auprès d'une grande nauf, laquelle
> ne se mouvoit, encores qu'elle eust pleine voile en haute mer:
> je croy bien que c'estoit celle de Periander, le tyran, laquelle
> un poisson tant petit arrestoit contre le vent.

So far, so good. But he adds at once, referring to Pliny's alleged eye-witness, 'Et en ce pays de Satin, non ailleurs, l'avoit veuë Mutianus' (ch. 29, p. 396). Likewise, the narrator scorns Pliny's account of elephants dancing on a tightrope, 'Là, non ailleurs, en avoit veu Pline, dansans aux sonnettes sus cordes, et funambules, (ch. 29, p. 393). Another tapestry scene shows Mediterranean wonders, including fish 'dansans, volans [. . .] chassans, dressans escarmouches, faisans embuscades, composans trefves, marchandans, jurans, s'esbatans' (ch. 30, pp. 398-99). The tapestry also shows earnest observers of this unlikely spectacle, with Aristotle to the fore, 'espiant, considerant, le tout redigeant par escrit' and behind him 'comme records de sergents, plusieurs autres philosophes' (p. 399). Scepticism reappears with the allegory of Ouy-dire and his pupils (ch. 30, p. 400). Ouy-dire, unable to move or see, verifies nothing for himself, he simply listens and repeats. His pupils include many modern and ancient authors, not least Herodotus, Pliny and Strabo. Chapters 29-30, then, pour scepticism on a range of ancient writers. It is particularly important to have evidence of such scepticism in an era which readily gave credence to the reports of ancient authorities. (On the status of Pliny in the early sixteenth century, see *10*, pp. 60-62; on Rabelais's attitude to ancient authorities, *7*, pp. 303-18.)

What are the implications for our understanding of the *Tiers* and *Quart Livre*? As they are discrete works, we cannot simply superimpose on them the scepticism of the *Ve Livre*; we may not, for example, assume that every allusion to Pliny is mocking. However, if the internal evidence suggests scepticism, then the *Ve Livre* may offer corroboration. One such case is *Tiers Livre*, chs 51-52, where, as we have seen, the narrator's blatantly exaggerated assertions of truthfulness suggest that he himself doubts some at least of the marvels which he records. Another relevant case is that of the unicorns which Pantagruel sends his father, with the remark,

> Je m'esbahis comment nos escrivains antiques les disent tant
> farouches, feroces et dangereuses [. . .] ferez espreuve du
> contraire; et trouverez qu'en elles consiste la mignotize la
> plus grande du monde. (*QL*, ch. 4, pp. 45-46)

Many, at the time, may have believed that unicorns existed, but not even Pantagruel was in a position to describe them from observation. What, then, is the force of his remarks? The simple answer seems to be that, as the plain meaning of his words suggests, this is another thrust at the authority of ancient writers. The reading is confirmed by the unicorn in the *pays de Satin*, for it is that specimen 'en tapisserie' which is termed a 'beste felonne à merveilles' (*VL*, ch. 29, p. 394). The main target here is probably Pliny (ib., n. 3).

Gaster's device to repel missiles (*QL*, ch. 62) is a harder case. He claims credibility for his invention on the strength of a list of supposedly analogous phenomena recorded by ancient authors. The list includes the remora (p. 228), whose reported powers are ridiculed in the *Ve Livre*. As we have seen, the narrator is silent on these wonders, and intervenes only to discuss the elder-wood flutes (p. 230). Interpreting silence is hazardous. However, given the evidence of *QL*, 4, and secondarily, that of *VL*, chs 29-30, a reader could reasonably take the narrator's silence to imply scepticism about the literal truth of the wonders cited by Gaster.

The heroes' visit to Medamothi, where they buy tapestries and pictures (*QL*, ch. 2), is illuminated rather similarly by reference to the *pays de Satin*. In one picture 'estoient au vif painctes les Idées de Platon, et les Atomes de Epicure' (p. 37). To talk of a painting showing 'au vif' the invisible is a joke, but is it against the philosophers or the painter? The use elsewhere of a tapestry to ridicule some fantasies of the ancients, including Aristotle and other philosophers (*VL*, ch. 30, p. 399), *suggests* that Plato and Epicurus are probably the main butt of the jest.

The scepticism of the *Ve Livre* is not confined to the Ancients. In Ouy-dire's audience are many 'modernes historiens cachez derriere une piece de tapisserie, en tapinois escrivans de belles besongnes, et tout par *Ouy-dire'* (*VL*, ch. 30, p. 401). They include travellers such as Marco Polo and Jacques Cartier, whose presence suggests scepticism about geographical and travel writing. Such incredulity has a bearing on the *Quart Livre*, and tends to confirm that some episodes may be read, at least partly, as parodies of travellers' tales. The episode of the Andouilles is one, the 'parolles gelées' another (see *25*). (For another view of relations between *VL*, chs 29-30 and the *QL*, see *23*, pp. 139-63; helpful on contemporary beliefs about unicorns.)

Legal satire exemplifies a second way in which the *Ve Livre* may illuminate the others, by revealing differences in emphasis. Mme Huchon dates the principal episode (*VL*, chs 11-15) from 1548 or soon after (*27*, p. 487). Most of the strictures are vehement in tone and radical in substance: the courts 'mynent et ruynent tout, sans discretion ['distinction'] de bien ou de mal [. . .] pillerie est leur devise' (ch. 11, p. 317). The text highlights one category of victims, the military nobility, the 'bons gentilshommes qui [. . .] s'exerseoient à la vollerie et à la chasse pour plus estre en temps de guerre escors ['skilful'] et ja endurciz au travail' (ch. 14, p. 326). In a bitter jest, Frere Jean suggests reasons why the Chats fourrez are so fond of game: they are still pursuing noblemen, even after death, for the souls of the latter will have transmigrated to the beasts which, in life, they had hunted:

> ces Chatz fourrez, avoir ['having'] leurs [. . .] possessions,
> rentes et revenuz destruit et devoré, encores leur cherchent-
> ils le sang et l'ame en l'autre vie. (ch. 14, p. 327)

Legal satire in the *Quart Livre* is, at first sight, similar. It is concentrated on the episode of the noble sieur de Basché, who is plagued, apparently without good cause, by bailiffs ('chi-

quanoux') acting for the 'gras prieur de Sainct Louant' (*QL*, ch.
12, p. 71). Basché solves his problem by having the Chiquanoux
beaten surreptitiously and so savagely that they finally leave him
in peace. The treatment of the topic in the *Ve Livre* might lead us
to expect unalloyed support for Basché's method of defending
himself. In fact, however, the comparison brings out the qualifi-
cations present in the *Quart Livre*. Criticism is restricted there to
the activities of local justices, 'ces juges pedanées soubs l'orme'
(*QL*, ch. 16, p. 85). And sympathy with Basché is not total, since
Epistemon has express reservations about his harshness to the
Chiquanoux (ib.). (On Basché, see *28*.) In short, comparison
with the *Ve Livre* highlights the relative balance of the *Quart* on
this point.

The courts' approach to truth is also handled distinctively in
the *Ve Livre*. Chapter 30 shows Ouy-dire 'tenant escole de tesmoignerie' (p. 389), and we learn that his pupils 'vivoient
honnestement du mestier de tesmoignerie, rendans seur tes-
moignage de toutes choses à ceux qui plus donneroient par
journée, et tout par *Ouy-dire*' (p. 402). Here the irony is
restrained. But when Grippeminault rants at Frere Jean, the
courts' scorn for truth is savagely caricatured:

> Pense tu estre en la forest Academicque avecques les ocieux
> veneurs ['hunters'] et inquisiteurs de vérité? Or sà, nous
> avons bien icy autre chose à faire, or sà: icy on respond, je
> dy, or sà, categoricquement, de ce qu'on ignore. Or sà, on
> confesse avoir faict, or sà, ce qu'on ne feit oncques. (ch. 12,
> p. 323)

It is instructive to contrast this passage with the treatment of justice in the *Tiers Livre*. That book certainly alludes to cruelty and
injustice committed by the judiciary, but dwells mainly on the
real difficulties of judgment. Comparison with the ferocious
satire in the *Ve Livre* brings out the measure and good humour of
the satire centred on Bridoye (*TL*, chs 39-44).

Our last example concerns literary manner. When the gover-
nor of Ruach talks about swallowing snakes, this exchange
ensues between Frere Jean and Pantagruel:

j'ay aultrefoys ouy dire que le serpens entré dedans l'estomach ne faict desplaisir aulcun, et soubdain retourne dehors,
si par les pieds on pend le patient, luy praesentant près la
bouche un paeslon plein de laict chauld.

– Vous, dist Pantagruel, l'avez ouy dire: aussi avoient
ceulx qui vous l'ont raconté. (*QL*, ch. 44, p. 169)

The exchange invites comparison with the allegory of Ouy-dire
(*VL,* ch. 30). (In passing, we may note a difference of content: as
Pantagruel goes on to cite an authority, that of Hippocrates,
against the hearsay remedy, our passage is less pervasively sceptical than *VL*, ch. 30.) If the passage is considered solely for its
form, it looks like a distillation into one peremptory rejoinder of
the whole allegory of Ouy-dire. Mme Huchon suggests (*27*, p.
485) that the chapters containing the allegory were probably
written by 1545, well before the *Quart Livre* appeared. If she is
right, it is likely that the allegory of Ouy-dire was indeed dis-
carded in favour of the version above. What makes this conjec-
ture interesting is that critics have stressed, no doubt rightly, the
increased predilection for allegory detectable in the *Quart Livre*
(e.g. *33*, p. 114). The apparent fate of Ouy-dire indicates that
allegory could still be sacrificed to dialogue. This observation
tends to support the idea that dialogue is a central feature of the
art of the *Quart Livre*. (See ch. 5, below.)

If used with due caution, then, the *Ve Livre* may provide
supporting evidence on the meaning, emphases, and literary
technique of the *Tiers* and *Quart Livre*. Full exploration of these
matters would of course go far beyond the scope of this book.

5

The Art of the Tiers Livre and Quart Livre

As this examination must be brief and selective, it concentrates on two essential features, direct speech and narration. Direct speech makes up about three-quarters of the *Tiers Livre*, three-fifths of the *Quart*; and the two works are rich in narration, both by the narrator and others. The narration is often in direct speech; this applies even to the narrator (e.g. in the Prologues). However, for clarity, I deal separately with narration, then with speeches and dialogue.

We have noted (ch. 1) that the narrator himself is explicitly present in some episodes, as when he says of the sibyl, 'je veidz qu'elle deschaussa un de ses esclos' (*TL,* ch. 17, p. 241). Often, the pronoun 'nous' implies his presence among the participants, e.g. 'Au cinquième jour [. . .] descouvrismes une navire marchande' (*QL*, ch. 5, p. 47). Admittedly, he sometimes reports the company's travels in the third person plural, e.g. 'decouvrirent une isle nommée Medamothi' (*QL*, ch. 2, p. 36). Though this use of the third person is slightly disconcerting, it does not rule out the narrator's presence as an onlooker. Thus, in the same chapter on Medamothi, 'nous' also occurs: 'Ce que sus tout trouvasmes' (p. 39). The narrator is, then, presented as having been a bystander at the very events which are the stuff of his books; he is himself a minor character within the fictional world of the *Tiers* and *Quart Livre*. The resultant narrative convention is that he is not omniscient and has no privileged access to knowledge; in principle, his grasp of events is not superior to that available to any other character, save that he has hindsight.

In keeping with these imaginary limitations, the narrator tells us little of the others' inner thoughts or feelings, and what he does tell us is usually associated with external signs. Typically, the statement that 'Panurge estoit fasché des propous de Her Trippa', simply anticipates Panurge's own words, 'Je me sens tout matagrabolisé en mon esprit des propous de ce fol endiablé'

(*TL*, ch. 26, p. 333), and does not imply narrator omniscience. Even if the source of the narrator's knowledge is unrevealed, it need not mean that he has privileged insight. He reports, for example, that Pantagruel colonized Dipsodie to keep it 'en [. . .] obéissance' (*TL*, ch. 1, p. 85); the narrator does not say how he knows this intention, but we may suppose that Pantagruel's reasons would be known in his entourage, to which the narrator belongs.

Sometimes the narrator teases the reader, by jocularly asserting the truth of plainly unbelievable stories, and daring him to disbelieve them. The most striking example concerns the Andouilles and Mardigras (*QL*, chs 38, 41), to which we shall return shortly. For now, it suffices to observe that these assertions, set among many other episodes which are, at the literal level, equally incredible, incline us to feel we are reading a collection of tall stories.

Thus, the narrator is presented as having restricted knowledge and some inclination to pull our legs. In one respect, this is immaterial: precisely because the events are often blatant whimsy, no reader can be much troubled about the narrator's veracity at the literal level. However, his limited credibility does matter in that it affects the authority of the judgments which he sometimes proffers. Just as his knowledge is not superior in kind to that of other characters, so too his judgments have no special weight. The point needs emphasis, since he goes by the seemingly authoritative name of 'François Rabelais'. Obviously, the narrator's views should not be discounted; rather, they must be assessed, like other characters' opinions, in the light of the rest of the text. For example, his praise of Pantagruel's wisdom (*TL*, ch. 2, p. 97) convinces because, generally, Pantagruel shows wisdom in contrast with Panurge's folly. But when the narrator declares it 'louable' that, on some feast days, the Papimanes display the Pope's portrait (*QL*, ch. 45, p. 171), the subsequent satire on their idolatry suggests that the praise is wrong or, more likely, ironic.

The narrator recounts the doings of Pantagruel and those around him, and also of some figures from outside their world, such as Galen (*QL*, Prologue, p. 12). In the *Tiers Livre*, narration

of either kind is subordinate to dialogue. For long periods, the
narrator merely punctuates the dialogue with such expressions
as '(dist Panurge)'. When he does narrate, it is sometimes to
describe the behaviour of characters consulted by Panurge, e.g.
the sibyl (ch. 17), Triboullet (ch. 45), Nazdecabre (ch. 20). These
cases do not reduce the primacy of dialogue, as the first two
characters' gestures may complement the meaning of their
words, and the mute Nazdecabre's are a substitute for speech. In
the *Quart Livre* the narrator relates more of the protagonists'
deeds, e.g. Panurge and Dindenault (ch. 8), the storm (chs 18-
19), the whale (chs 33-34), the Andouilles (chs 35-36, 38, 40-
41), Panurge's conduct off Ganabin (ch. 67). Additionally, he
tells of the fall of the Guaillardetz (ch. 45). We may first consider the Andouilles, because of the distinctive tone that the narrator imparts to the episode.

This account of warlike sausages serves the pleasures of the
tall story. After two preliminary chapters, including the unlikely
advance of the 'puissantes et gigantales Andouilles [. . .]
furieusement en bataille marchantes vers nous' (ch. 36, pp. 145-
46), the narrator spends a chapter affirming the truth of his tale.
He opens, 'Vous truphez ['mock'] ici, beuveurs, et ne croyez que
ainsi soit en verité comme je vous raconte' (ch. 38, p. 152). Like
references to drinking elsewhere in the book (e.g. ch. 1, pp. 33-
34; ch. 10, p. 64), the term 'beuveurs' evokes conviviality and
good humour. The expression 'Vous truphez' reflects one of the
pleasures of listening to a tall story, i.e. scoffing at it. The narrator goes on, 'Croyez le, si voulez; si ne voulez, allez y veoir.
Mais je sçay bien ce que je veidz. Ce feut en l'isle Farouche. Je
la vous nomme' (ib.). This line of defence, a challenge from an
alleged eye-witness to visit an exotic place and see for ourselves,
serves to emphasize that it is specifically travellers' tales which
are being parodied here. (This may be the clearest glimpse, in
the *Quart Livre*, of the scepticism about such accounts which
pervades the *pays de Satin*, *VL*, ch. 30.)

The narrator next defends his claims by citing other examples of the Andouilles' powers. The supposed parallels include
the Garden of Eden: 'le serpens qui tenta Eve estoit andouillicque: ce nonobstant est de luy escript qu'il estoit fin et

cauteleux sus tous aultres animans. Aussi sont andouilles' (p. 153). The other analogies are similarly extravagant.

The narrator presents his analogies jokingly, as in this piece of mock-servility, 'Si ces discours ne satisfont à l'incredulité de vos seigneuries' (ib.). This mocking attitude reappears particularly in chapter 41. Relating the slaughter of the Andouilles, the narrator says, 'Et dict le conte que si Dieu n'y eust pourveu, la generation Andouillicque eust [. . .] toute esté exterminée' (p. 162). The words 'dict le conte' may be a jocular echo of a formula apparently common in medieval prose narratives; *Melusine,* for example, to which the narrator himself alludes (p. 153), uses expressions such as 'l'istoire nous dit . . .' three times in four pages (Jehan d'Arras, *Melusine,* ed. Ch. Brunet, Paris, Jannet, 1854, pp. 18, 20, 21). More importantly, the formula 'dict le conte' implies that our narrator is using some other narrative source, despite his claim to report as an eye-witness. The inconsistency is blatant mockery of the reader, for it heralds the entry of Mardigras, the flying pig.

These passages, then, emphasize the pleasures of a kind of imaginary dialogue between readers and narrator: on the readers' side, the pleasure of sociable scoffing; on the narrator's, that of mocking his readers and impudently upholding the incredible.

This interplay between narrator and audience does not exhaust the comedy. The humour of the episode lies partly in the characters' divergent reactions. Faced with the Andouilles and the equally startling 'Saulcissons à cheval', Pantagruel 'feut en grand esmoy, et non sans cause' (ch. 36, p. 146). Frere Jean, however, dismisses the threat: 'Ce sera icy une belle bataille de foin ['unreal']' (ch. 39, p. 154). He offers to fight the Andouilles with the aid of the cooks, does so successfully, and thus makes Pantagruel's apprehension look ridiculous.

Pantagruel's officers, Riflandouille and Tailleboudin, also deserve attention. Epistemon thinks their names promise victory, should the Andouilles attack (ch. 37, p. 148). Pantagruel agrees, and then discourses, in more general terms, on the possibility that proper names may have prophetic or other significance. He lists several cases from Antiquity which seem to support this view; and though he does not explicitly endorse it, he shows no scepticism. However, the comic-sounding names Riflandouille and Tailleboudin raise doubts. More particularly, their associations invite our scepticism. Riflandouille is an executioner in the medieval *Mystère de saint Quentin* (*3*, p. 333) and also a companion of Loup Garou in *Pantagruel*, ch. 29. Tailleboudin (Talhebudin) is an adversary of Lent in a play written for Carnival revels by Jehan d'Abundance, *Le Testament de Carmentrant* (ca 1540; in *16*). These names, then, have unheroic connotations, unlike those which Pantagruel cites from Antiquity, e.g., Regalianus (or Regillianus) chosen as Emperor 'par signification de son propre nom' (ch. 37, p. 149). Any allegation of an analogy is thus incongruous. Similar incongruity attends any attempt to draw parallels between epoch-making events in Antiquity (including Augustus's becoming Emperor) and this 'bataille de foin'. The officers' names and the burlesque occurrences in which they take part seem a gentle parody of the theories sketched by Pantagruel in chapter 37, and invite reservations about them. (On the linguistic implications, see *34*.)

Thus, while this episode may raise what was for contemporaries a serious point about meaningful names, it exemplifies primarily a style of narration unique to the narrator; other characters tell stories, but none adopts this tone or attitude to his audience. These chapters also offer one of the few hints, in the *Tiers* or *Quart Livre*, of laughter at Pantagruel. Since the narrator is a character, it makes sense to talk of his having moods; we may say, therefore, that it is as if a mood of self-assertion leads him both to mock his readers and also make fun of his hero.

Other aspects of the narrator's art may be illustrated from his account of Diogenes at Corinth (*TL*, Prologue, pp. 63-69). The story falls roughly into halves: one on the Corinthians ('Quand Philippe [. . .] au combat couraigeuses', pp. 63-67); the other on Diogenes ('Diogenes, les voyant [. . .] cessateur et ocieux', pp. 67-69). Each half has three parts. For the Corinthians, we find an opening statement of the threat which prompts action: 'Quand Philippe [. . .] leur ville defendre' (p. 63). There follows a list of the men's activities: 'Les uns [. . .] retiroient [. . .] chascun desrouilloit son bracquemard' (pp. 63-67). Finally comes a sentence on the women's activities:

> Femme n'estoit, tant preude ou vieille feust, qui ne feist four-
> bir son harnoys: comme vous sçavez que les antiques
> Corinthiennes estoient au combat couraigeuses. (p. 67)

Mention of their reputation recalls that in Antiquity they were
known mainly for their immorality. The expression 'fourbir son
harnoys' has a literal military sense but, applied to these women,
is an erotic metaphor. The metaphorical use brings out retrospec-
tively the erotic connotations of some of the expressions applied
to the men: 'chascun desrouilloit son bracquemard' takes on
clear sexual overtones, as do the 'pistoletz' and 'viroletz' of the
previous paragraph (p. 65). Impliedly, the men are not occupied
solely at military tasks. The closing lines, then, counterbalance
what precedes with an unheroic gloss on the Corinthians' apparent martial zeal.

The account of Diogenes, too, opens with a few lines on
what leads to his activity: 'Diogenes, les voyant [. . .] comme
excité d'esprit Martial' (p. 67). Then his acts are listed: 'ceignit
son palle [. . .] qu'il ne le defonçast' (pp. 67-69). Finally, we
have further explanation from Diogenes himself: 'Ce voyant
[. . .] pour [. . .] n'estre veu seul cessateur et ocieux ['idle']' (p.
69). That explanation, ostensibly about saving appearances,
undermines the opening allusion to 'esprit Martial'.

Both halves, then, follow the same pattern: heroic explanation, activities, unheroic explanation. Each half ends in anticlimax. The identical progression of the halves is a formal counter-
part to the unflattering parallel which we saw Diogenes draw
between the Corinthians' behaviour and his own (ch. 2).

By their length, the lists of activities dominate the narration.
They differ slightly in composition. The narrator writes of the
Corinthians, as if giving an exhaustive enumeration of arms and
structures. There is only one hint of items omitted, 'scorpions, et
autres machines . . .' (p. 65). The impression of exhaustiveness
is particularly strong because several groups of nouns denote
things which are distinct, but generically akin, and which could
easily be summarized. For example, 'rancons', 'hanicroches',
and 'parthisanes' (p. 65) all denote arms in the halbard family.
Alongside this plethora of items, Diogenes's actions are few, but

the narrator conveys them by numerous synonyms. Thus, 'croul-loit', 'barattoit', 'bransloit', 'esbranloit' (p. 67) all imply one action, shaking. It is as if the narrator is deliberately amplifying both lists, but more obviously the second, far beyond what is needed to give the basic information.

One function of these extended enumerations is to reduce to the same level all the actions listed. Indeed, it is probably true of both lists that their sheer length is the main factor in levelling down all the actions recorded. However, the levelling is further due to uniform presentation, with little narrator intervention. Thus, 'remparoient murailles, dressoient bastions' (p. 63) and 'assoyoient sentinelles, forissoient patrouilles' (p. 65) have, for-mally, much the same weight, even though the first pair of expressions refers to major building operations, the latter to minor troop movements. True, the narrator does briefly highlight some actions. He devotes two lines to Diogenes's flattening a piece of ground, and judges the outcome a 'belle esplanade' (p. 67). But the prominence so bestowed is then obliterated by the sixty-four verbs relating Diogenes's treatment of his tub. It seems, there-fore, that the narrator's inflation of the lists and very limited comments tend to reduce the acts reported to a mere concatena-tion of syllables, and thus help him to suggest yet further the futility of those endeavours.

The lists differ in one major way. The first is orderly, deal-ing in turn with provisioning, fortifications, horse armour and personal armour, missiles, shafted weapons, and side-arms. Also, the actions recorded seem consistent. Not so, in the case of Diogenes, whose acts are aimless. Typically, he nullifies his labour in bringing the tub uphill by pushing it back down, and he lavishes on the tub both care ('nattoit [. . .] flattoit') and ill-treatment ('tabustoit [. . .] tracassoit'). Elsewhere, he treats it inappropriately: for example, he uses a wood-plane on it ('vreloppoit'), even though it is made of clay, and covers it as if it were a horse ('caparassonnoit'). Finally, the order of verbs sometimes appears inspired rather by similarity of sound than any relationship of sense, e.g. 'levoit, lavoit, clavoit'. There is, then, a contrast between the Corinthians, whose seemingly coherent acts are enumerated coherently, and Diogenes, whose incoherent acts are reported incoherently. We have already seen that, as regards content, the parallel drawn between the Corinthians and Diogenes discredits the former. We have also seen that the narrations of their acts and of his follow similar trajectories into anticlimax; the similarity emphasizes the parallel in content. As for the contrast just noted, that between seeming coherence and flagrant incoherence, it makes the report of Diogenes's actions a distorting mirror held up to mock the Corinthians.

The use of parallels and divergences in this story illustrates a subtler aspect of the narrator's art than the self-advertising raillery with which he carries off the Andouilles episode. (In passing, it must be said that not all lists are used so precisely and meaningfully; some, though not meaningless, seem loose and too long, e.g. when Panurge addresses Frere Jean (*TL*, ch. 26, pp. 333-39), or Xenomanes describes Quaresmeprenant (*QL*, chs 30-32).)

We now turn to story-telling by other characters, who mainly recount anecdotes about figures not otherwise present in these books, e.g. Pope John XXII and the nuns of Coingnaufond (*TL*, ch. 34, pp. 415-17). For present purposes, an 'anecdote' is narrative (it relates a sequence of events), and self-contained. The characteristic of being narrative distinguishes anecdote from mere report of memorable sayings, such as the rejoinders of Diogenes (*QL*, ch. 64, p. 235) or the servant-girl (*TL*, ch. 35, pp. 427-29). The characteristic of being self-contained distinguishes anecdote from allusion, that is, from passages which are fully comprehensible only if the reader knows the outside source to which reference is made; examples of allusion are Panurge's reference to Leander's prayer (*TL*, ch. 26, p. 341) and Frere Jean's to his own defence of the abbey of Seuillé (*QL*, ch. 23, p. 110). As there are several marginal cases, counting the anecdotes is rather arbitrary. Very tentatively, therefore, I should say that there are thirty anecdotes told by characters in the *Tiers Livre*, thirty-nine in the *Quart*. Two occupy several chapters each: Basché and the Chiquanoux, narrated by Panurge (*QL*, chs 12-15); and the story of the peasants and the devil (*QL*, chs 45-47), told by an anonymous 'on' (p. 177). Others are very short: fifteen occupy ten lines or fewer. But the majority of the others (thirty-nine) cover 11-30 lines. (For consistency, I have used *4* for counting lines in both works.) The anecdotes are sufficiently long and numerous to be notable features of both the *Tiers* and *Quart Livre*. Apart from the two very long examples, their presence is most marked when they occur in groups (e.g., *TL*, chs 19, 33, 34; *QL*, chs 11, 52).

Usually characters tell anecdotes to support a view on a subject under discussion. Thus, Pantagruel tells of Seigny Joan to exemplify the sound judgment of the *fou* (*TL*, ch. 37, pp. 447-51), and Frere Jean recounts the prank played on the seigneur de Guyercharois to excuse his own discourtesy (*QL*, ch. 10, pp. 65-66). Some tales are less apposite than others, but the pure digression is rare. A possible example is Panurge's story about a Bishop of Auxerre, which pertains to the Church calendar or clerics' love of wine, but not the subject of the moment, cuckoldry (*TL*, ch. 33, pp. 407-09).

Telling amusing stories is also part of the characters' conviviality. An attempt may be made to divert, even when a serious point is involved. Thus, while Panurge seems persuaded that the story of Basché really illustrates a 'remede tresbon' for those plagued by litigious churchmen and their agents (*QL*, ch. 12, p. 71), he means also to amuse, witness Pantagruel's comment, 'Ceste narration [. . .] sembleroit joyeuse' (*QL*, ch. 16, p. 85). There are of course more obviously entertaining stories, such as those appearing in the heroes' 'menuz devis' (*QL*, ch. 11, pp. 68-69). These particular tales have also a mildly competitive aspect. Pantagruel having told the story of Antagoras, Panurge caps it with another on the same theme, 'Je dameray ceste cy . . .' Here exchange of brief anecdotes is part of the dialogue, a reminder that anecdote cannot be treated in complete isolation from dialogue and other uses of direct speech.

In these works, anecdote is essentially an art of concision. A good specimen is the story of the deaf-mute Verona, told by Panurge, to show that women interpret all gestures as erotic (*TL*, ch. 19, pp. 263-65). He opens by setting the event in a long time-scale ('ce que advint en Rome deux cens Ix ans après la fondation d'icelle'), suggesting that it will be historically significant. And what is the event? It is that Verona, having misconstrued a passer-by's gestures, the two, 'sans de bouche mot dire, feirent beau bruit de culletis'. The narrative is a comic anticlimax. It depends on economy and appositeness in the information given. For example, we learn of the nameless hero that he is a 'gentil-homme' (implying social standing), and that he is asking about senators (suggesting some interest in public life); these two points taken together conform to the apparent gravity of the opening sentences. Otherwise, we learn simply that he is young, which helps explain the outcome of the episode. Comparable economy marks the account of gestures. The man's signs, which Verona mistakenly thinks amorous, are crucial. Panurge terms them, quite abstractly, 'gesticulations italiques', relying on his hearers' imagination to supply the detail. Of Verona's gestures, which she intends to be erotic, Panurge says:

> par signes (qui en amour sont incomparablement plus attrac-
> tifz, efficaces et valables que parolles) le tira à part en sa
> maison, signes luy feist que le jeu luy plaisoyt.

Again, Panurge does not detail the gestures, but concentrates on their meaning and results. Though the parenthesis '(qui [. . .] parolles)' may seem otiose, it offers an explanation of the speed with which the man is seduced. The story is a fine example of succinct comic bathos, achieved by strict relevance and a partic-ular use of abstraction to obtain economy. (The abstraction con-trasts interestingly with the narrator's lengthy, concrete account of gestures in chapter 20; there the details are needed because Panurge and Pantagruel are to disagree about their meaning.) The story is typical of the Panurge of the *Tiers Livre* in involv-ing sex and a cynical view of morality, especially women's morality. Being expertly told, it is also typical of Panurge the entertainer.

The question of typicality clearly pertains not only to charac-ters telling stories but to all cases in which they express them-selves in direct speech. To the broader question of direct speech we now turn. Characters sometimes speak at length, for thirty lines or more. (This is obviously an arbitrary length; I choose it only because it marks the upper limit for most anecdotes.) I can consider just two examples. The first is Pantagruel's defence of Bridoye (*TL*, ch. 43, pp. 503-07).

Pantagruel first clarifies the capacity in which he addresses the Court, as petitioner rather than judge ('Messieurs [. . .] lieu de suppliant' p. 503). He goes on to put three legal arguments in Bridoye's favour ('En Bridoye [. . .] diroit salée', pp. 503-05), then a religious one ('Et me semble [. . .] humbles', p. 505). Having used argument, he changes approach and simply asks, as a favour to himself, that Bridoye be exonerated, on certain conditions ('Je mettray [. . .] judiciaires', pp. 505-07). Finally, he asks for the use of Bridoye's services, if the Court still insists on removing him from judicial office.

Pantagruel's argued case rests expressly on authorities. He refers first to the law itself: 'vous entendez [. . .] quelle facilité de pardon [. . .] nos loix oultroyent'. Then he cites biblical authority: 'Dieu [. . .] comme sçavez, veult souvent sa gloire apparoistre en l'hebetation des saiges [. . .] et en l'erection des simples et humbles' (after I Corinthians I. 27). In each case, he professes, not to teach the judges, but to highlight points which they know already. This is a modest and tactful use of authorities, consistent with the role of supplicant in which Pantagruel casts himself.

A similar remark applies to the following section. At the start of the chapter, the presiding judge Trinquamelle had spoken to Pantagruel of the 'obligation [. . .] en laquelle vous tenez par infinis biensfaictz cestuy parlement' (p. 503). But when Pantagruel comes to ask, as a favour to himself, that Bridoye be excused, he says,

> vous priray, non par celle obligation que pretendez à ma maison, laquelle je ne recongnois, mais par l'affection syncere que [. . .] avez en nous congneue. (p. 505)

The personal favour is indeed being sought in return for something. However, that something is not tangible benefits, but simply the goodwill shown to the Court by Pantagruel and his ancestors. The distinction may seem spurious, in that the benefits are a practical result of the goodwill. But in principle the differ-

ence is considerable. To rest the plea for leniency on past benefits and on the 'obligation' which allegedly arises from them is
to restrict the Court's freedom. On the other hand, mere goodwill
creates no obligation, and leaves the Court free to refuse leniency. Pantagruel's distinction between benefits and 'affection
syncere' is thus part of his respect for the Court. Likewise, in
requesting Bridoye's services, should the Court remove him
from office, Pantagruel modestly recognizes that the Court may
reject his representations on Bridoye's behalf.

The speech is clearly constructed. The transition from argument to appeal is marked, for example, by the device of preter-
ition, 'Je mettray en obmission toutes ces choses' (p. 505). The
step from Pantagruel's appeal to his contingency position of asking for Bridoye's services is heralded by the weighty conjunction
'En cas que' (p. 507). Preoccupation with clarity also emerges in
Pantagruel's way of itemizing the content of his speech. For
example, 'plusieurs qualitez' become 'Premierement vieillesse,
secondement simplesse [. . .] tiercement [. . .] un aultre cas'.

In other respects, too, the speech exhibits precision. We have
already seen that, in content, several important distinctions are
made explicitly. The concern with nuance extends into the
details of vocabulary, as one example will show. To make legal
points, Pantagruel uses *reconnaître,* appearing to connote certainty: 'je recongnois un aultre cas [. . .] en noz droicts deduict';
'celle obligation [. . .] laquelle je ne recongnois'. But on the
mysteries of divine intervention, he uses the tentative *sembler*:
'Et me semble qu'il y a je ne sçay quoy de Dieu' (p. 505). The
first sentence of the legal argument is comparable: 'En Bridoye
je recongnois plusieurs qualitez, par lesquelles me sembleroit
pardon du cas [. . .] meriter'. Pantagruel applies *reconnaître*
to features whose existence is certain (e.g. Bridoye's age).
However, he uses *sembler* of the judgment to be based on these
features, since he is not speaking as a judge, but a petitioner.
The tentative use of the conditional 'sembleroit' marks the same
distinction. Thus precision of thought shapes vocabulary and,
on occasion, syntax too.

The speech has little adornment. However, Pantagruel does
use two images to buttress his legal arguments. First, he speaks

metaphorically of Bridoye's impeccable earlier record as the 'mer immense de tant d'equitables sentences', which will wholly absorb his one bad decision (p. 505). Then he reverses the image, so that the wrong decision itself becomes a drop of sea-water which would vanish in a great river: 'si, en la riviere de Loyre, je jectois une goutte d'eaue de mer, pour ceste unique goutte [. . .] personne ne la diroit salée'. Referring to familiar things and resting on simple analogies, these images accord with Pantagruel's self-effacing approach. Nevertheless, it is notable that the second image is strictly redundant, for it adds nothing substantive to the first. Even here, then, there is a hint of a tendency to a more ample manner. Also, the reversal of the initial analogy between sea-water and sound decisions indicates a liking for pattern-weaving. The same part of the speech shows some other signs of a more expansive manner, notably the accumulation of verbs, 'estre abolie, extaincte et absorbée' and the pair of parallel main clauses which are the culmination of the sentence, 'personne ne la sentiroit, personne ne la diroit salée'. However, given that this is a speech, it is clear that such repetitions produce the kind of emphasis which can assist listeners, and are not *mere* decoration.

What should we conclude about this speech? It is measured in content and respectful in tone. The modest approach, whereby the speaker tries to coax rather than coerce his hearers into acquiescence, looks very persuasive. Pantagruel shows good organization, precision and just enough emphasis. It is fine oratory. (Which need not mean that it is successful; the text does not tell us.) We may feel also that the temperate approach and clarity of thought are characteristic of the serene Pantagruel, who 'jamais ne se tourmentoit' (*TL*, ch. 2, p. 97).

Our second example is a speech in an ample manner, Panurge's argument (*TL*, ch. 8) that the cod-piece is the 'premiere piece de harnoys pour armer l'homme de guerre' (*TL*, ch. 7, p. 147). (Here 'premiere' seems to refer both to importance and chronology.) For present purposes, it is enough to consider one paragraph, 'Voyez [. . .] sus toutes bestes' (ch. 8, pp. 149-51). The first two sentences deal with Nature's intention that species breed to survive, and the protection therefore provided for the reproductive parts of plants. The third and last sentences deal with man who, being originally destined for peaceful mastery of plants and beasts, had no need of such protection and so was not provided with it by Nature. The paragraph, then, is built round the contrasting natural provisions made for plants and for man. About two thirds are devoted to plants, one third to man. Since the difference is due largely to the two lists of examples which Panurge gives in the section on plants ('gousses [. . .] echines poignans' and 'poix [. . .] toutes plantes generalement'), the imbalance reflects the multifarious generosity of Nature to plants, as against the comparatively niggardly treatment of man.

Let us now look more closely at the opening sentence:

1) Voyez

2) comment nature

P) voulent les plantes, arbres, arbrisseaulx, herbes, et zoophytes, une fois par elle créez, perpetuer et durer en toute succession de temps, sans jamais deperir les especes, encores que les individuz perissent,

2) curieusement arma leurs germes et semences,

2r) es quelles consiste icelle perpetuité

3) et les a muniz et couvers par admirable industrie de gousses, vagines, testz, noyaulx, calicules, coques, espiz, pappes, escorces, echines poignans,

3r) qui leurs sont comme belles et fortes braguettes naturelles.

Syntactically, its skeleton is the main clause (1), and the pair of noun clauses (2 and 3) coordinated by 'et'. Each noun clause is accompanied by an explanatory relative clause (2r and 3r). Clauses 2 and 2r stand in parallel to 3 and 3r. The structural parallel reinforces the sense that 2, 2r, 3, and 3r form a unit. This in turn helps to counterbalance the bulky parenthesis (P), which separates the subject of 2 and 3, 'nature', from its finite verbs 'arma' and 'a muniz'.

In substance, the parenthesis is fundamental, because it states Nature's intentions, 'voulent les plantes [. . .] durer [. . .] sans jamais deperir les especes'. The erudite neologism 'zoophyte' and the sheer mass of botanical examples in the parenthesis (and in 3) have an air of learning and so of authority. Internally, the parenthesis is a web of pairs of expressions, some complementary, some antithetical. Thus, 'perpetuer et durer' is complemented by 'sans jamais deperir'; 'une fois' is set antithetically against 'en toute succession de temps', the fate of the 'especes' against that of the 'individuz'.

The noun clauses express the provisions which Nature makes: 'arma leurs germes [. . .] les a muniz [. . .] de gousses . . .' There is progression between the two clauses, in that 3, giving examples of natural 'armour', specifies the sense of 'arma' in 2. The explanatory relative clauses connect Nature's actions to her intentions. Clause 2r, ending with 'perpetuité', strongly echoes a key word in the parenthesis ('perpetuer'). Clause 3r, according to which plants' pods and so forth 'leurs sont comme [. . .] braguettes naturelles', carries Panurge's argument decisively forward: while again linking nature's actions and intentions, it simultaneously asserts the analogy between these overridingly important natural defences and the cod-piece; this is the point at which he seeks to put the authority of Nature itself behind his claim for the primacy of the cod-piece.

As a whole, then, the sentence is copious in examples, remains reasonably clear and balanced in syntactic structure, and carries its argument elegantly forward. And no doubt similar observations could be made about the rest of the paragraph and of the speech. The oratory here is skilful and erudite. It also seems typical of Panurge. Certainly, unlike Pantagruel's speech examined above, it is highly assertive, as witness the number of expressions tending to preclude disagreement ('L'exemple y est manifeste'; 'voyons apertement') and perhaps even in the use of the imperative 'Voyez' to open the demonstration. Again, where Pantagruel seeks to base his claims on authorities, Panurge argues a case which is ostensibly his own. (Some of the material comes unavowedly from Pliny.) And where Pantagruel proceeded by careful distinctions and a couple of clearly articulated analogies, Panurge indiscriminately accumulates large numbers of examples, possibly disparate (e.g. 'gousses' and 'echines poignans') and slips in his analogy with the one word 'comme'.

Lastly, we turn to dialogue. I define 'dialogue' as any exchange of words between two or more characters. The exchanges may include longish speeches (e.g. *TL*, ch. 5; *QL*, ch. 53). The definition also takes in the 'blason' passage, in which Pantagruel and Panurge alternately suggest adjectives to describe Triboullet and so build up a list several pages long (*TL*, ch. 38, pp. 453-61). Equally, it covers brief snatches of repartee, as between Pantagruel and Panurge on the expression 'vendre parolles' (*QL*, ch. 56, p. 207).

A rough classification of these dialogues is possible. First, they may be classified according to whether or not they are functional. 'Functional' dialogues are those which serve mainly to initiate new episodes, as when Pantagruel invites Panurge to consult Hippothadée and other experts (*TL*, ch. 29), or to give background information, as when Xenomanes tells his companions of Quaresmeprenant and his enmity with the Andouilles (*QL*, chs 29, 35). Non-functional dialogues, conversely, are those which seem to exist mainly for their inherent interest; often they are set-piece discussions, e.g. on divine providence (*TL*, ch. 30) or deaths of Heroes (*QL*, ch. 26). At times, the distinction is only a matter of degree. Some dialogues are 'functional' in that they introduce new episodes, but they also include quite substantial discussion. For example, a debate on the nature of language is involved in reaching the decision to consult Nazdecabre (*TL*, ch. 19), and a discussion on prophecy (*TL*, ch. 16) precedes the visit to the sibyl.

An alternative classification distinguishes between 'dramatic' and 'non-dramatic' dialogues. In the former there is interaction between characters: for example, they may try to dominate or manipulate one another, or simply fail to understand one another. The more obviously disputatious examples include debates of prophecies about Panurge's marriage (e.g. *TL*, chs 12, 14, 18, 20), in which he seeks to impose his views willy-nilly. Other noteworthy dramatic dialogues include his first consultation about marriage with Pantagruel (*TL*, ch. 9) and his encounter with Her Trippa (*TL*, ch. 25). Instances in the *Quart Livre* include Panurge and Dindenault (chs 5-7), part of the storm (chs 19-22), or the travellers and Homenaz (chs 49-54). Non-dramatic dialogues, on the other hand, are simply exchanges of information or opinion, without competition or other involvement of personalities, e.g. the dispassionate discussion of prophetic names (*QL*, ch. 37).

The two classifications – functional / non-functional and dramatic / non-dramatic – are alternatives, but obviously they do not exclude one another. Thus, we might classify as both non-functional and dramatic almost any of the dramatic dialogues listed in the previous paragraph. It should also be stressed that these classifications have little inherent significance, and certainly imply no value-judgments; a 'dramatic' dialogue, for example, is not necessarily better than a 'non-dramatic' one. I propose these distinctions merely to draw attention to some salient features of dialogues in the works. One other general point may be made. Some dialogues involve exercises in linguistic virtuosity, e.g. the 'blason' (*TL*, ch. 38) or, less markedly, Panurge's first consultation, which is built partly round Pantagruel's alternating replies, 'Mariez-vous doncq' and 'Poinct doncques ne vous mariez' (*TL*, ch. 9). Such virtuosity can occur in any of the categories of dialogue identified above.

We may now look more closely at an example of a non-functional dramatic dialogue, Panurge's questioning of Trouillogan on his marital prospects (*TL*, chs 35-36). Trouillogan is a 'philosophe ephecticque et pyrrhonien' (ch. 36, p. 431), i.e. a sceptic with a reasoned belief that nothing can be known for sure. Accordingly, his answers are largely non-committal. For example, rather than give unqualified positive or negative answers, he will introduce fresh alternatives:

> PANURGE. Et si je ne marie poinct?
> TRO. Je n'y voy inconvenient aulcun.
> PANURGE. Vous n'y en voyez poinct?
> TRO. Nul, ou la veue me deçoit ['deceives']. (ch. 36, p. 431)

His caution can become ludicrous. We know that he has remarried (ch. 29, p. 371). Yet, when asked whether he is married, and whether he has been married before, Trouillogan answers respectively, 'Il me l'est advis' and 'Possible est' (ch. 36, p. 437). Another foible is pedantic literalness. When Panurge makes an assumption for sake of argument, 'Mettons le cas que je sois marié', Trouillogan asks, 'Où le mettrons-nous?' (ch. 36, p. 435). Such excesses make Trouillogan a caricature of the sceptic. In part, this is a criticism of a useless philosophy, witness Gargantua's impatience with him (ch. 36, p. 439). At the same time, however, the caricatural excesses create a distinctive literary character, and are surely tolerable for the few pages that he takes up.

Moreover, Trouillogan is not purely ridiculous. In particular, his very pedantry means that he uses words carefully. If we weigh his answers, it becomes clear that some are more substantial than they appear. When first asked whether Panurge should marry or not, he replies, 'Tous les deux' and 'Ne l'un ne l'aultre' (ch. 35, p. 425). Panurge thinks the answers self-contradictory, but Hippothadée and Pantagruel judge them capable of clear interpretation, and also satisfactorily consistent with the teaching of St Paul (ch. 35, p. 429). When Panurge pleads, 'Mais, conseillez moy, de grace. Que doibs je faire?', Trouillogan answers, 'Ce que vouldrez' (ch. 36, p. 429). Though the reply looks curtly dismissive, it is sound advice: Panurge must, literally, do what he wants. Certainly, that coincides with Pantagruel's advice that Panurge must decide for himself (ch. 10, p. 167; ch. 29, p. 367). Thus, though indeed a caricature, Trouillogan has worthwhile things to say.

However, Panurge believes him merely evasive. This belief shapes the dialogue between them, particularly in chapter 36, in which he questions Trouillogan closely. The philosopher is reticent longer and more obviously in this chapter; at moments, he simply declines to answer, saying for instance, 'je m'en excuse' and even 'je n'en peu mais' (pp. 433-35). Such responses suggest that he feels he has already said all that he has to say. The deadlock ends only when Panurge yields to frustration: 'Par la chair, je renie [. . .] je renonce. Il m'eschappe' (p. 439).

Panurge's closing sentence indicates his approach in this dialogue. He frames his questions to try and trap the philosopher into giving him a plain answer. His efforts at entrapment and Trouillogan's reactions – either evasive, or else meaningful, but in a way which eludes Panurge – make the dialogue a genuinely dramatic verbal joust. One example may suffice. In chapter 35, the major question was cast as a choice of alternatives, 'Panurge se doibt il marier, ou non?' (p. 425). Trouillogan, in each of his answers, responds to both halves of the question, either accepting both alternatives ('Tous les deux'), or rejecting both ('Ne l'un ne l'aultre'). As we have seen, these answers satisfy Pantagruel, but not Panurge, who thinks that, by avoiding questions phrased in the alternative (disjunctives) he will force a plain answer. He tells Trouillogan: 'Je parleray d'aultre style [. . .] parlons sans disjunctives, ces membres mal joinctz vous faschent, à ce que je voy [. . .] me doibs-je marier?' (ch. 36, p. 431). For a time he manages to avoid giving alternatives, but still does not secure replies that satisfy him. Consequently, seeking a new tack, he asks Trouillogan about his own marriage: 'Attendez. Puisque de cestuy endroict ne peuz sang de vous tirer, je vous saigneray d'aultre vene. Estes vous marié ou non?' Unfortunately, in seeking a new line, he has forgotten the disjunctive pitfall, and back comes the inevitable response, 'Ne l'un ne l'aultre, et tous les deux ensemble' (*2*, p. 251; the text of *1*, p. 437 is slightly inaccurate). The exchange is doubly comic. As regards Trouillogan, his reply is so immediate and seemingly mechanical as to fit perfectly Bergson's definition of comedy, 'du mécanique plaqué sur du vivant' – human beings abruptly behaving like machines. As for Panurge, the philosopher's answer comically deflates his hopes for his new line of questioning. And, by echoing the response given to his main question in chapter 35, these words recall economically that he has received his answer already, if only he had had the wit to heed it. The new anticlimax thus underlines the personal foolishness which is fundamental to Panurge the comic character. Perhaps, too, this dialogue offers a variation on the idea that the seemingly futile, here an exchange of what sounds like mere verbiage, may be instructive to those who, like Pantagruel and Hippothadée, are wise enough to perceive its significance.

Our second dialogue is part of the travellers' reception by the Papimanes: 'Incontinent qu'ilz feurent joinctz à nostre nauf [. . .] le monde plus Pape n'auroit' (*QL*, pp. 179-81). The Papimanes seek news of the pope from the heroes; the latter are perfectly willing to give it; what fills the dialogue with comic misunderstandings (and makes it 'dramatic' in our sense) is the blundering impatience of the Papimanes.

The Papimanes' behaviour implies eagerness. They set out to meet the travellers, 'soubdain que nos ancres feurent [. . .] jectées' (p. 179), and start asking questions without ceremony, the instant they are alongside. The four Papimanes are of one mind. From the start, they speak in chorus, 'tous ensemble' (ib.), reflecting their common obsession with the pope. They assume their obsession is shared by the seafarers; otherwise, they could not expect the question 'Le avez vous veu [. . .] l'avez vous veu' (ib.) to be understood to refer to the pope. The same goes for other terms, such as 'celluy là', which they later use (ib.). The Papimanes' questions thus show them besotted with their obsession. The fact that they speak in chorus probably heightens the effect by making them seem mechanical; certainly, it suggests that they have no individuality and are incapable of independent thought. The Papimanes' questions form a crescendo, in that the terms designating the pope grow in extravagance: 'le' is followed first by the still neutral 'celluy là', but then by 'l'Unicque', by 'celluy qui est' (p. 180), an expression which in the Bible means God Himself, and finally by the unequivocal 'Dieu en terre' (ib.). The crescendo then subsides into comic bathos when Panurge claims to have seen three of these unique beings and thus staggers the Papimanes, who cannot grasp unaided that he means, 'les uns successivement après les aultres' (ib.).

The following paragraph ('Adoncques se agenoillerent . . .'), which is partly narrative, goes on from the Papimanes' verbal excesses to the servile gestures by which they propose to greet anyone who has seen the pope, and the startling welcome which they would bestow on the pontiff himself, 'Nous luy baiserions le cul sans feuille, et les couilles pareillement' (p. 180). These words do more than underline the Papimanes' folly. When they call the Pope 'celluy qui est', Pantagruel protests that 'Celluy qui est [. . .] est Dieu [. . .] Oncques certes ne le veismes, et n'est visible à œilz corporelz' (p. 180). The transcendent nature of his God is thus emphasized. By contrast, the Papimanes' intended welcome for the pope, concentrating on what is most fleshly and human, reveals the latter's mere humanity in a degradingly carnal way.

The part played by the heroes in the passage is secondary, but important. Each one who answers the Papimanes' questions speaks in character. Frere Jean responds impulsively, and thinks at once of violence: ' ". . . je l'assommeray de coups", pensant qu'ilz se guementassent de quelque larron, meurtrier ou sacrilege' (p. 179). The offer is amusingly at odds with the treatment which the Papimanes have in mind for the pope. Epistemon's answer is polite and reasonable, 'Seigneurs [. . .] exposez nous, s'il vous plaist, de qui entendez, et nous vous en dirons la vérité' (ib.). Again, this is typical of the character, witness his measured verdict on Basché and the Chiquanoux (*QL*, ch. 16, p. 85), or his debate with Panurge during the storm (*QL*, ch. 21, pp. 102-03). The answer also contrasts with the obscure clamourings of the Papimanes. Pantagruel's answer is theological, and rests typically on biblical authority, 'en tel mot [Dieu] se declaira à Moses' (p. 180; cf. Exodus III. 14). Panurge replies assertively, and with an indication of disappointed self-interest: 'Ouy, ouy [. . .] ouy dea, messieurs, j'en ay veu troys, à la veue desquelz je n'ay gueres profité' (p. 180). Neither the assertiveness nor the self-interest is surprising. The diversity of the travellers contrasts with the uniformity of the Papimanes, and each character, by responding in his own way, serves to highlight an aspect of the Papimanes' limitations. It also shows again how consistently the former are characterized in the dialogues and other direct speech passages.

The remarks above are not a systematic study of the art of the *Tiers* and *Quart Livre*. However, they may offer some indication of the quality of the texts in varying types of narration, oratory, and dialogue. The books exhibit a wide range of manners, from the abundantly expansive to the laconic; the former is no doubt the predominant tendency, but the latter is commoner than might be imagined, particularly in the telling of anecdotes. But perhaps more important than mere range of manners is the fact that, as a rule, these different manners have precise functions in creating characters and upholding certain values.

Bibliography

The following includes only a minute fraction of the work published on Rabelais, and perforce omits many excellent studies. Because of the obscurities of the texts, I have given some priority to informative works over critical ones.

ABBREVIATIONS

BHR = Bibliothèque d'Humanisme et Renaissance.
ER = Études Rabelaisiennes.

EDITIONS

1. *Tiers Livre*, edited by P. Michel, Collection Folio (Paris, Gallimard, 1966).
2. *Tiers Livre*, edited by M. A. Screech (Geneva, Droz, 1964).
3. *Quart Livre*, edited by R. Marichal (Geneva, Droz, 1947).
4. *Œuvres complètes*, edited by P. Jourda, 2 vols, Classiques Garnier (Paris, Garnier, 1962).
5. *Œuvres complètes*, edited by G. Demerson and others, Collection l'Intégrale (Paris, Éditions du Seuil, 1973). Contains useful translations into modern French.
6. *Gargantua and Pantagruel,* translated by Sir Thomas Urquhart and P. le Motteux, edited by D. B. Wyndham Lewis, 2 vols, Everyman's Library (London, Dent, 1929). Free but useful seventeenth-century translations of all five books.

GENERAL STUDIES

7. R. Antonioli, *Rabelais et la médecine* (Geneva, Droz, 1976). Ranges beyond technical matters.
8. M. Bakhtine, *L'Œuvre de François Rabelais et la culture populaire au Moyen Âge et sous la Renaissance,* translated by A. Robel (Paris, Gallimard, 1970). Accepted neither by all scholars nor in its entirety, but influential on the focus of much recent work.
9. M. A. Screech, *Rabelais* (London, Duckworth, 1979). Illuminates the context, in ancient and Christian thought, of most episodes considered in this book.

On Chapter 2

10. J. Céard, *La Nature et les prodiges: l'insolite au XVIe siècle* (Geneva, Droz, 1977).
11. L. K. Donaldson-Evans, 'Panurge *perplexus*: ambiguity and relativity in the *Tiers Livre*', *ER*, 15 (1980), 77-96. Intelligent iconoclasm.
12. J. Calvin, *Advertissement contre l'astrologie judiciaire*, edited by O. Millet (Geneva, Droz, 1985).
13. V.-L. Saulnier, 'L'Enigme du pantagruelion ou: du *Tiers* au *Quart Livre*', *ER*, 1 (1956), 48-72. Helpfully reviews earlier interpretations of *pantagruelion*.
14. M. A. Screech, *The Rabelaisian Marriage* (London, Arnold, 1958).
15. L. Schrader, 'Panurge: théories récentes, observations méthodologiques, conséquences possibles', *ER*, 21 (1988), 145-56. Surveys work on Panurge from 1953 to 1984.

On Chapter 3

16. *Deux jeux de Carnaval de la fin du Moyen Âge*, edited by J.-C. Aubailly (Geneva, Droz, 1977).
17. E. Cameron, *The Reformation of the Heretics* (Oxford, Clarendon Press, 1984).
18. M.-M. Fontaine, 'Quaresmeprenant: l'image littéraire et la contestation de l'analogie médicale' in *Rabelais in Glasgow*, edited and published by J. A. Coleman and Christine M. Scollen-Jimack (Glasgow, 1984).
19. J. Jacquart, *François Ier* (Paris, Fayard, 1981).
20. F. Joukovsky, 'Quelques sources épicuriennes au XVIe siècle', *BHR*, 31 (1969), 7-25.
21. L. Romier, *Les Origines politiques des Guerres de Religion*, 2 vols (Paris, 1913). Useful on the *crise gallicane*.
22. M. A. Screech, 'Sagesse de Rabelais, Rabelais et les "bons christians" ', *ER*, 21 (1988), 9-15.
23. P. J. Smith, *Voyage et Ecriture: étude sur le 'Quart Livre' de Rabelais* (Geneva, Droz, 1987). Reflects manifold recent studies.
24. E. V. Telle, 'L'Ile des alliances ou l'anti-Thélème', *BHR*, 14 (1952), 159-75.
25. T. Tornitore, 'Interpretazioni novecentesche dell'epidosio delle *Parolles Gelées*', *ER*, 18 (1985), 179-204. Critically surveys work on this episode.

On Chapter 4

26. A. Glauser, *Le Faux Rabelais* (Paris, Nizet, 1975).
27. M. Huchon, *Rabelais grammairien* (Geneva, Droz, 1981).

28. R. Marichal, 'Rabelais et la réforme de la justice', *BHR*, 14 (1952), 176-92.
29. G. A. Petrossian, 'The Problem of the Authenticiy of the *Cinquiesme Livre de Pantagruel*', *ER*, 13 (1976), 1-64.

On Chapter 5

30. D. G. Coleman, *Rabelais* (London, Cambridge University Press, 1971).
31. A. C. Keller, *The Telling of Tales in Rabelais* (Frankfurt am Main, Klostermann, 1963).
32. D. N. Losse, *Rhetoric at Play: Rabelais and satirical eulogy* (Bern, Frankfurt am Main, Las Vegas, Peter Lang, 1980). Informative on background, interesting analyses.
33. F. Moreau, *Un aspect de l'imagination créatrice chez Rabelais: l'emploi des images* (Paris, SEDES, 1982).
34. F. Rigolot, 'Cratylisme et Pantagruelisme', *ER*, 13 (1976), 115-32.

ADDENDA

35. J. E. G. Dixon and J. L. Dawson, *Concordance des Oeuvres de Rabelais* (Geneva, Droz, 1992).
36. K. M. Hall, *Rabelais: 'Pantagruel' and 'Gargantua'* (London, Grant & Cutler, 1991). On Rabelais's earlier works.

CRITICAL GUIDES TO FRENCH TEXTS

edited by
Roger Little, Wolfgang van Emden, David Williams

1. **David Bellos.** Balzac: La Cousine Bette.
2. **Rosemarie Jones.** Camus: L'Etranger *and* La Chute.
3. **W.D Redfern.** Queneau: Zazie dans le métro.
4. **R.C. Knight.** Corneille: Horace.
5. **Christopher Todd.** Voltaire: Dictionnaire philosophique.
6. **J.P. Little.** Beckett: En attendant Godot *and* Fin de partie.
7. **Donald Adamson.** Balzac: Illusions perdues.
8. **David Coward.** Duras: Moderato cantabile.
9. **Michael Tilby.** Gide: Les Faux-Monnayeurs.
10. **Vivienne Mylne.** Diderot: La Religieuse.
11. **Elizabeth Fallaize.** Malraux: La Voie Royale.
12. **H.T Barnwell.** Molière: Le Malade imaginaire.
13. **Graham E. Rodmell.** Marivaux: Le Jeu de l'amour et du hasard *and* Les Fausses Confidences.
14. **Keith Wren.** Hugo: Hernani *and* Ruy Blas.
15. **Peter S. Noble.** Beroul's Tristan *and the* Folie de Berne.
16. **Paula Clifford.** Marie de France: Lais.
17. **David Coward.** Marivaux: La Vie de Marianne *and* Le Paysan parvenu.
18. **J.H. Broome.** Molière: L'Ecole des femmes *and* Le Misanthrope.
19. **B.G. Garnham.** Robbe-Grillet: Les Gommes *and* Le Voyeur.
20. **J.P. Short.** Racine: Phèdre.
21. **Robert Niklaus.** Beaumarchais: Le Mariage de Figaro.
22. **Anthony Cheal Pugh.** Simon: Histoire.
23. **Lucie Polak.** Chrétien de Troyes: Cligés.
24. **John Cruickshank.** Pascal: Pensées.
25. **Ceri Crossley.** Musset: Lorenzaccio.
26. **J.W Scott.** Madame de Lafayette: La Princesse de Clèves.
27. **John Holyoake.** Montaigne: Essais.
28. **Peter Jimack.** Rousseau: Emile.
29. **Roger Little.** Rimbaud: Illuminations.